Third Edition

HOUSE RABBIT
HANDBOOK
How to Live with an Urban Rabbit
BY MARINELL HARRIMAN

DROLLERY PRESS

To Herman and Phoebe
and their successors

Drollery Press, Alameda
Published in association with David Lewis.

Photographs by the author, plus
additional photographs by Amy Espie
and others, as noted.

Printing by Quebecor Printing, Kingsport.
Design by Bob Harriman.

Library of Congress Cataloging-in-Publication Data

Harriman, Marinell, 1941–
    House rabbit handbook : how to live with an urban rabbit / by
Marinell Harriman. — 3rd ed.
        p.   cm
    Includes bibliographical references (p.   ) and index.
    ISBN 0-940920-12-3
    1. Rabbits. 2. Rabbits—Anecdotes. I. Title.
SF453.H37 1995
636'.9322—dc20   95-33183
                                                      CIP

Drollery Press
1524 Benton Street
Alameda, California 94510

CONTENTS

PREFACE

THE FIRST EDITION OF HOUSE RABBIT HANDBOOK was to acquaint you with the concept of "house rabbit," an unknown term in 1985. My intention was to prove that rabbits could live in human houses. To verify this point, I used a preponderance of evidence in the stories of many rabbits living in human households.

By the time the second edition of *House Rabbit Handbook* was published, the House Rabbit Society, a nonprofit rabbit rescue organization, was formed. Information could be obtained not only from homes with one or two rabbits but also from foster homes where numerous rabbits could teach their humans about rabbit behavior and health.

In the third edition, I no longer need to prove that rabbits can be wonderful indoor companions and family members. Many thousands of people who live with rabbits are making this fact public. The question now is not, Can it be done?

but rather, How well can it be done?

The intention of this book is to help make the sharing of a human home a joyful experience for both the animals and the humans who dwell within that home.

As rabbit rescuers and fosterers, my husband and I have shared living space with hundreds of different rabbits during the past ten years. We have met a wide variety of personalities and have dealt with major and minor health problems. Some of our earliest rescued rabbits are still with us, and they have taught us a great deal about the various stages in a rabbit's life. We've even experienced moving into a new neighborhood, taking with us the forty-one rabbits we had at that time.

ACKNOWLEDGMENTS

I often call *House Rabbit Handbook* the book that writes itself—due to the tremendous support in concept and content from the dedicated people behind it.

House Rabbit Society volunteers across the country, who turn their lives upside down to rescue rabbits and educate people, provide the "stuff of experience" used in this book.

A note of thanks for copy editing goes to: Amy Espie, Beth Woolbright, Betty Tsubamoto, Holly O'Meara, Margo DeMello, and Sandi Ackerman—who helped me shape the content of this edition. Amy Espie's photographic contributions are taken directly from animals fostered in her home.

We are extremely grateful to the professionals who gave time reviewing and editing material that required specific expertise: Carolynn Harvey, DVM; Richard Evans, DVM, MS; Barbara Deeb, DVM, MS; Karl Waidhofer, DVM; Susan Smith, PhD; and William Harriman, PhD.

PHOTOGRAPHS, ABOVE: MARINELL HARRIMAN, OPPOSITE PAGE: AMY ESPIE; INSERT: BOB HARRIMAN

First get acquainted with the general
characteristics of the species.
Then you can better meet the needs of
the individual rabbits who share your home.

Dan Donahue (inset) and Kelisha

THE MENTAL MAKEUP

WHAT A GREAT SURPRISE it is to new rabbit people that they have an intelligent creature in their midst with an inquisitive mind that is constantly looking for activity. Rabbits are comprised of paradoxes that make them extremely entertaining—inquisitive yet cautious, skittish yet confident, energetic yet lazy, timid yet bold.

Being *crepuscular*, not nocturnal, rabbits are most active at dawn and twilight. They spend a long mid-day "down time," during which they usually seek the solitude of a cage or quiet corner for a nap. This habit fits the schedule of working people who are away from home part of the day. Rabbits will adapt well into any consistent human routine.

Living low to the ground (floor, carpet), they are clumsy in high places. Yet, their explorations may take them from inside the closet, behind the sofa, or under the bed to the heights of dressers, desktops, and tables. (Solid footing is required for the loftier investigations.) A single youthful rabbit can lay waste to the contents of accessible shelves, delighting in pulp fiction and the daily news. And the clatter heard from the kitchen is most likely due to pots and pans being rearranged.

High-minded exploration:
Hopping with compulsive curiosity from bed to dresser, Herman stops to reflect.

WITTY AND WILY

Rabbits solve problems, like pushing on doors that open outward and pulling with their teeth on doors that open inward. They learn to use a litterbox, to come when they're called, and to sit up and beg for a treat. They have a remarkable ability to remember furniture arrangements and where tasty snacks are usually kept.

They can learn procedures and routines at any age. Smart animals that they are, rabbits play games—with toys, with other animals, and with their humans. They play games of their own invention, punctuated by sudden vertical leaps and 180° turns in mid-air.

Consistent with those of other animals, rabbits' games mimic sur-

PHOTOGRAPH: MARINELL HARRIMAN

"...when allowed some freedom, rabbits perform beyond their supposed capacity."

vival techniques. Just as predatory animals enjoy chase games, rabbits more often play getaway games. Sometimes carrying a prized possession (such as a cracker), one may run from imagined thieves. Or after yanking an envelope from a human hand, a frisky rabbit zigzags off with a "catch-me-if-you-can" dare to pursuers. And on many occasions, witnesses have observed rabbits playing follow-the-leader.

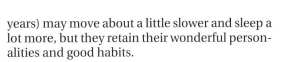
Literary pursuits: *Elevated tastes push a youthful Trixie beyond the lower shelve's required reading.*

AGE OF INNOCENCE

In terms of conforming to human standards of acceptable indoor behavior, a rabbit's age of innocence is at maturity. Most rabbits don't reach their full potential for a relationship with humans until after their first year. By this time too many humans have discarded them.

The stage of intense curiosity, hyperactivity, and frantic chewing and digging occurs at the height of adolescence (4-8 months)—a time that we recommend neutering or spaying. During adolescence, or preferably before, a house rabbit's environment should be thoroughly bunny-proofed, and plenty of litterboxes should be available (details in chapter 3).

Some of the rabbits we rescued years ago were never adopted into new homes and have continued to live with us. As they settled in, they became very easy to manage and very mellow. (All are spayed or neutered.) Our seniors (over 6 years) may move about a little slower and sleep a lot more, but they retain their wonderful personalities and good habits.

FREEDOM TO PERFORM

Like other animals when allowed some freedom, rabbits perform beyond their supposed capacity. The key here is opportunity. What individual expression can you expect from an animal who never gets out of a cage?

One year, we were passing out educational papers at a pet fair. Our booth displayed examples of rabbit toys and a photo collection of house rabbits doing their normal things. A man stopped at our booth and exclaimed, "Wow! I didn't know rabbits could do all of this! Ours is in

"Rabbits who live in our houses take up our habits."

a hutch in our backyard, and she just sits there."

Newly enlightened, the man went home to turn his hutch rabbit into a house rabbit, and we celebrated her victory.

Rabbits who live in our houses take up our habits. Like us, they are preoccupied with appearances and are meticulous groomers. They engage in household activities with other occupants. They learn many human words. They can distinguish their name, as well as, "Come," "Box," "Outside," "Yum," "Let's go," and a number of endearing terms and sweet nothings mentioned in the right tone of voice. Rabbits make a big effort to learn our language. It's our turn to learn theirs. ■

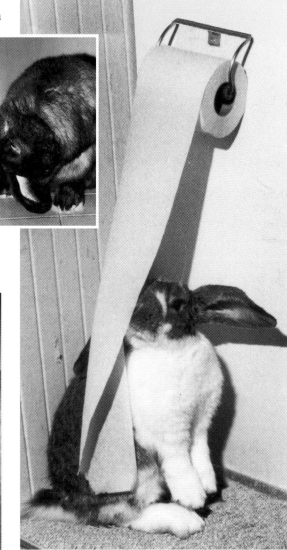

Just Routine: *Patrick does some serious ear washing (inset) while Daphne wipes her face in jest (right). Darla's daily ritual is a game with her human.*

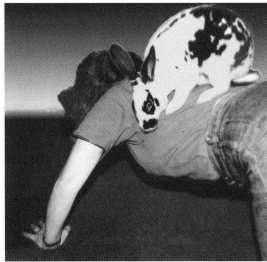

PHOTOGRAPHS, LEFT: DON LATARSKI, RIGHT, INSET: MARINELL HARRIMAN

RABBIT-SPEAKE

WHEN WE FIRST STARTED to "rabbit school" we learned some basic vocabulary. With time, we are refining our education and even learning a little rabbit poetry along the way.

Scientific observations of wild rabbits give us background data on rabbit behavior. When we live with rabbits, we watch them closeup and listen to what they are saying when they "speak" to humans. In living with different people, rabbits develop different "dialects," which are best understood by those who live with them and love them.

Just as in our own language, we have homonyms (the same word with different meanings) so do rabbits. The important thing to bear in mind is context.

A BODY OF INFORMATION

Most rabbit "words" are communicated by action. Others are transmitted simply by posture. Happy postures include whole-body smiles of several kinds.

The peaceful stretch. Bunny flattens out on his belly with hind feet extended straight out. Upon occasion, toes may curl under, or the feet may cross at the ankles.

The sideways flop. If you find your bunny flopped over on his side or back, it does not mean he has had a heart attack. The fluttering eyelids and whiskers indicate that bunny is contentedly in dreamland.

Presentation, another smile, in the horizontal position, is assumed by the recipient of petting by a favorite human or grooming by another animal. All feet are tucked under, while the chin is laid out flat on the floor. This is how subordinate rabbits "present" themselves to their superiors. But a presentation is also used as voluntary submission to a loved one, meaning something like: Take me. I'm yours (see page 44).

Crouching is a tense unrelaxed version of presenting, usually with bulging eyes, in which the rabbit is not enjoying attention but rather frozen in fear.

The shudder. This is a comical whole-body expression. If your hands emit an obnoxious odor—like too much perfume or carburetor cleaner—when you pet your bunny, he may try to

Lapin laughter *is unmistakable in The Bun's joyful wake-up yawn (left).*

Phoebe's phonetics of the feet (above) stand for happiness, friendship, comfort, and a general sense of well-being.

PHOTOGRAPHS, LEFT: WRENN DABNEY REED, RIGHT: TANIA HARRIMAN

"A rabbit who licks a human hand is not just trying to get salt..."

shake it off. Sometimes after a rabbit is given medicine, he may shake his coat to rid himself of the bad taste.

WORD OF MOUTH

Another "word" with two different definitions is tooth grinding.

Purring. This is a series of fast but light vibrations of the teeth and happily quivering whiskers—activated by gentle stroking behind the ears. It signifies contentment to the Nth degree.

Crunching. The second meaning is one of discomfort, expressed by a sick animal. Tooth crunching is usually a louder slower grind, sometimes with protruding eyes. Context will help you distinguish a happy grind from a painful crunch.

The whimper is a fretting little noise made by a pregnant or pseudo-pregnant female, who is pleading not to be disturbed. Some rabbits whimper when you try to pick them up or pull them from their cage.

Wheezing sniffs. Other rabbits "voice" a protest by combining vocalizations with nasal sounds.

Clucking. A pleasant sound is the faint *clucking* made by a bunny who has been given a particularly tasty snack. It always means, Yum, yum!

LOVE AND WAR

Rabbits are very intense over friends and enemies and use obvious language to address them.

Licking/grooming. This is obvious affection. A rabbit who licks a human hand is not just trying to get salt—as some people who are unfamiliar with rabbit talk may believe. What a silly idea! Rabbits don't lick each other because they crave salt. Rather, they crave affection.

Honking/oinking. Because rabbits draw very little distinction between sexual and social behavior, many expressions are identical. Neutered males and spayed females may still court—circling each other (or your feet). Soft honking or oinking is a love song, also used to solicit food and attention. A honk can mean: I want you, or maybe a treat

Nudging/huddling. More ways to show affection involve sitting close. These friendly gestures are often overlooked by humans. Instead of licking, many house rabbits nuzzle nose-to-nose with their human friends. Nudging your ankle or tugging on your pantleg means, Notice me.

Nipping. This is not necessarily an angry remark. Happily bonded pairs use it all the time simply to mean, Move over. With humans it sometimes means, I'm scared of heights. Put me down.

Snorting/growling. In anger this may be just a warning or it may coincide with a grunt-lunge-bite directed at an adversary. This kind of anger is predictable and can be prevented (see page 35).

TALL TAILS AND ASSERTIONS

Most of the time you are seeing only the tip of bunny's tail, which looks like a small cotton ball—until something excites her.

"Menacing, tightly pulled back ears say, Watch out!"

Body talk: *Phoebe has sassy words for one cat, yet endearing words for a different cat..*

Erect tail. The excitement shown by a tall erect tail can be caused by the threat of an adversary, the proximity of a potential lover, anticipation of tasty treats, or simply the appearance of a new toy.

Tail twitching. In a competitive or a courting context, rabbits may twitch their tails from side to side and spray their conquests. A modified assertion is simply tail-twitching as a form of "back talk."

Ear assertions. Ears send and receive messages. Alert *forward ears* say, I hear you. Alert *bi-directional ears* say, I hear you and something else, too. Menacing, tightly *pulled back ears* say, Watch out!

Chin assertions. A benignly assertive gesture is chinning, a peculiar way of claiming property. By rubbing their under-chin scent glands on the items, they mark them as possessions(undetectable to us).

FEET NOT ON THE GROUND

In addition to smiling, feet may kick, dance, thump, or take a variety of actions.

Kicking. In protest, kicking is high and to the back. In play or combat, rabbits kick to the side.

PHOTOGRAPHS: TANIA HARRIMAN

"Nature has designed rabbits—through shape and wiliness—to thwart predators."

Dancing. You'll know it when you see this frolicking series of sideways kicks and mid-air leaps accompanied by a few head shakes and body gyrations. Many rabbits have literally danced their way into human affection.

Thumping. This has several meanings: I detect something out of the ordinary, or I have an announcement to make.

Rabbits thump over many things—sights, sounds, smells, and things that we don't sense. It might be a danger signal, and then again it might not be. You might be warned of "danger" that the furniture has been rearranged.

Yet, this sense of propriety is the very thing that can make a rabbit a highly suitable individual to share your home.   ∎

Point of View

BETH WOOLBRIGHT

GWENDOLYNN IS THE ONE *who taught me how the world can look to a prey animal. Naturally, with other rabbits I'd wondered what they saw and how they viewed their world. And, depending on context, all rabbits can be wary. But never before had I imagined the perspective that Gwendolynn helped me to see.*

A stray with a permanent limp when she moved in, Gwendolynn had an unabiding distrust of humans, even as she delighted in exploring the safe environs of the house. A hand in her cage sent her whipping in circles to avoid being touched. Other rabbits had taught me the immeasurable value of patience. Although a few bunnies are carefree, most require that you first earn their trust.

I had read in HRS articles that the way to befriend an aloof bunny is to sit on the floor of a small room and then ignore the rabbit. It worked. On my stomach on the floor, I read a book. Gwendolynn hopped on my back, until I peeked at her, and then she disappeared. Of course, as a prey animal, she'd be aware of eyes. Walking down the hall, if I covered my eyes she wouldn't bolt. She'd watch me.

Nature has designed rabbits—through shape and wiliness—to thwart predators. How they're shaped influences how they move and react. With short front legs and muscular back ones, they hop in quick unpredictable patterns, which can make them tough to catch if they're not ready to go back to their room or cage.

Their heads and eyes are shaped to notice movement in the distance, but they rely more on the nose for objects close to the face. It took me years to realize that Patrick, a round-faced lop, lunged at my wavering hand because it scared him; he didn't seem to recognize what it was. When I learned to put my fist on the floor he'd nudge me for pets, and he stopped attacking.

Unlike cats or rats, as ground dwellers (and not tree climbers), nervous rabbits are not designed for holding on when in someone's arms. On an instinctual level, how different is being scooped up and cradled from being carried off in a dog's mouth or snatched away in an eagle's talon? It takes a lot of trust on a rabbit's part (or a human with lots of confidence) to feel at ease in such a vulnerable position.

Whether Gwendolynn's wariness was based on nature or past experience, I'll never know. In not pursuing her too fast and spending lots of time with her, I have been successful in earning her trust. Now, she greets me at the door and sniffs me up and down. She will even let me pet her—if she's sandwiched between Bugsy and Tina, her two bunny bodyguards, that is.   ∎

HERMAN'S PLACE

ERMAN WAS A GIRL. The fact that we named her Herman should give you some idea how little we knew about rabbits (e.g. how to determine their gender) when she hopped into our yard in 1981. By the time we discovered our error, she had learned her name, which suited her just fine.

I have told Herman's story so many times that you might think the computer has "hung up." Yet, I have come to realize that Herman is a symbol. She is the experience that changed the way many people think of rabbits. Letters from all over the world re-live this experience—of the first rabbit and human ignorance that turned into knowledge. "This was my Herman," I am reading on the backs of enclosed photos.

When we first met Herman, my husband assumed he would build a hutch in the backyard, but we would keep her in the kitchen until then. The hutch was never built.

During our house takeover, we held another crazy notion—that our bedroom was not a bunny room. We had not reckoned with a rabbit who could open doors and sneak into our bedroom and become so exhilarated over her victory that she would turn our bed into a trampoline. Amused, we let her have it during the day. We continued to put her in the kitchen at night, while she continued to insist on sleeping with us. It took another six months before she won. We had to adjust to having our faces licked every ten minutes all through the night. It did occur to me to turn over, but I would usually find that she was standing on my hair (all fourteen pounds of her) and had me pinned to the pillow.

FAIR AND PROPER TREATMENT

Herman demonstrated a remarkable sense of fairness in the equal distribution of petting, grooming, and licking. She would shove her head under Bob's hand when it was his turn to pet her. I can't claim that she actually counted, but after a given number of strokes, it was her turn to groom him again.

Animals are not necessarily child substitutes. Sometimes it's the other way around. Herman was often a parent, or a grandparent. She may not have wiped away tears with her apron, but she could certainly soothe and comfort us and assure us that things were OK.

In seeing that things were properly done, Herman supervised all household activities from fixing the washer to sorting out magazines. Propriety could be mixed with mischief, and

PHOTOGRAPH: MARINELL HARRIMAN

newspapers were grabbed from startled readers' hands. It soon became apparent, after we chased her around the room, that it was the attention she wanted, not the paper. "You cheat," I often told her. "You manipulate me with your charms, and it's not fair."

At times she was downright sneaky, revealing her guilt with her tail. I might have walked by her unaware that she had pulled a book from the bookshelf, until I saw her tail twitching defiantly.

A SENSE OF HUMOR

I was taken by surprise when Herman accepted my invitation to play. I crouched down and wiggled my fingers ghoulishly and said, "I'm going to *get* you." With that information, she kicked up her heels and playfully flung her huge frame from side to side for the whole length of our living room, leaving me in gaping astonishment. "She gets it!" I said. "She really gets it!"

MEANINGFUL LIVES

Because her time with us was short, only two and a half years, we had to find out why. In the course of learning better rabbit-care, we have met many other people who are motivated by the same kind of loss and work toward the same goals. In tribute to these wonderful rabbits who have determined our cause, we seek improvements in the lives of others of their kind.

Herman's place in "rabbit history" is that of catalyst in a "movement" that demands consideration, respect and quality care for rabbits. Without Herman there would be no *House Rabbit Handbook*, and there would be no House Rabbit Society to rescue rabbits and educate people across the country. The door that Herman opened stays open as long as her work is being done and people's hearts are being captured.   ∎

Ecstasy of two kinds: After a hard day's work, Herman indulges in total relaxation (left) or an extra helping of parsley from her drawer (right).

PHOTOGRAPHS, ABOVE: BOB HARRIMAN, OPPOSITE PAGE: AMY ESPIE

Adoptable rabbits come in all shapes. A successful adoption is not due to picking the bunny with the "best" personality but rather to setting up an environment that brings out the best in the bunny you do bring home.

Foster rabbit Barney.
Kim Stiewig (inset) reading a
House Rabbit Journal.

PLANNING FOR A NEW FAMILY MEMBER

THERE IS MUCH EMPHASIS on choosing the right rabbit. People shop, scrutinize, consider, poke and probe, check teeth, coat, and temperament, and then make an emotional decision. I no longer encourage people to look for the "right" rabbit. It's too easy to believe, at the first difficulty, that you have chosen the wrong rabbit.

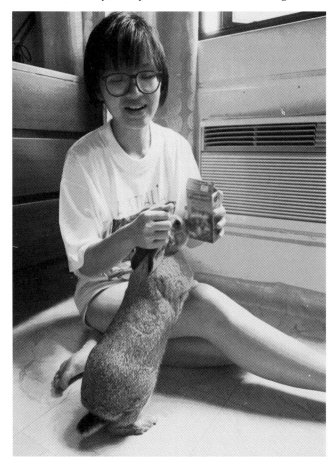

Or worse yet, you may blame the rabbit for not fitting your expectations. I once selected a "wrong" rabbit. I felt disappointed and guilty. This rabbit grew up to be my marvelous Phoebe, one of the greatest joys our home has ever known.

YOUR QUALIFICATIONS

There are many right rabbits, and every rabbit can be the right rabbit if appreciated for her own intrinsic virtues. The success and happiness of a relationship with a house rabbit depends rather on the *right people*.

Before setting out on a search for the right rabbit, test yourself to see if you are qualified to live with one or more of these wonderful animals.

■ Do you have a sense of humor?
■ Are you willing to learn rabbit talk? Can you take time to watch and listen?
■ Are you willing to make some compromises in your furniture arrangements?
■ Are you willing to do more vacuuming than you would in a rabbit-less home?
■ Are you willing to follow safety rules?
■ If your family is of varying ages, are you willing to supervise children's activities with the rabbit and be responsible for the rabbit yourself?
■ Will you take your bunny with you when you move to a new location?

If you qualify in those areas, that's a good start. Willingness must be present before you can follow through on any of the procedures that will make your relationship mutually rewarding. Instead of insisting that your new housemate meet all of *your* needs, concentrate on learning about and meeting your bunny's needs.

What kind of needs? *Bunnies do not need treats in their diet. If you give them for psychological reasons (e.g. to establish friendship), limit them to low-calorie, high fiber varieties.*

PHOTOGRAPH: QUAK WAN-LING

"Why should it be necessary for children to pick up the family rabbit?"

CONSIDER THE SIZE

Breed purity and youth are not prerequisites for a marvelous companion. Litterbox training is even easier with an older rabbit. My own breed recommendations are very general, but I will point out a common misconception. No matter what cute calendar photos you have seen, small children and rabbits are not the best combination.

Parents often think they want a small bunny that their children can pick up. A far better choice, especially if the family includes toddlers, is a rabbit with some heft that the kids cannot pick up. Parents don't expect children to pick up and carry the family dog. Why should it be necessary for children to pick up the family rabbit?

If your family includes children under 7 years old, think in terms of working with both rabbits and children. Unless you are willing to spend a lot of time supervising, it would probably be best to wait until the child is older.

On the other hand, I'm not suggesting that if you already have a rabbit and are expecting your first child that you should get rid of your rabbit. With some commitment, many parents have been able to set up living arrangements that are safe, rich, and rewarding for both rabbit and child.

CONSIDER THE ENVIRONMENT

Before bringing your bunny home consider the living and running space. Rabbits are burrowing animals who do not consider their cage a prison but rather a safe place for naps. Even the most adventurous rabbit welcomes the security of a cage to use as headquarters. Think about where you want to put a nice roomy cage. It should be where you spend a lot of time: next to your bed? Your desk? Your phone? This does double duty in socializing. The cage area should be quiet but not too quiet. It should be active but not

A lot of bunny to love: Size teaches its own lesson—that rabbits can be fully enjoyed without being lifted and carried.

too active.

All happy homes, both rabbit and human, contain some variety. We don't want so much peace and quiet that we are bored, and we don't want so much excitement that we are constantly stressed. There should be plenty of natural light but not direct sunlight. Temperature at 60°–75° is comfortable for a rabbit, but more cold than heat can be tolerated.

DEALING WITH THE UNPLANNED

It's always best to make decisions in advance when expanding your family with both human and non-human members. But if you should so happen upon a stray rabbit who needs a home, try working backwards and educate yourself in rabbit care. It may be unplanned, but it might be the beginning of something wonderful. ∎

PHOTOGRAPH: HUGH DOUGLAS

Preparing Bunny's Habitat

THE MINUTE YOU DECIDE to adopt a rabbit, start saving your old newspapers. You will need them to line cage trays. Next, shop for and collect the other necessities.

THE CAGE SETUP

Even if you plan to design and build a fancy habitat later, it's often easier to start with a ready-made cage. You and your bunny can decide on its best features. The size of the cage should be influenced by the amount of time spent inside it. A general rule for long-term use is 3-4 times the (stretched out) body length. If you have a baby bunny, then think of the adult size or plan to replace your starter cage with a larger one.

The cage should have large doors—side opening for bunny's convenience and top opening for your convenience. You can always add or enlarge doors. Your pet supply store may customize your cage for you, or you can modify it yourself with supplies from a catalog.

Convenient setup: A side door is added to this top-opening cage, along with hanging bottle, feeder, and rug.

FURNISHINGS AND SUPPLIES

Most of the articles needed to set up a cage and starter space can be found in pet supply and feed stores. Other items can be found in hardware, variety, import, and toy stores.

Water crock/bottle. Purchase crocks or heavy clay bowls from pet-product suppliers. Designer pottery from other sources may contain lead.

Hanging water bottles take up less space and make better use of limited space in starter cages.

Pellet crock/hanging feeder. Where space is not a problem, crocks can be used for food as well as water. Heavy clay is preferable to lightweight plastic. Plastic bowls should have wide lips that can't be gripped in bunny's teeth and turned over.

A hanging feeder, like a water bottle, allows more floor space inside the cage. This usually requires cutting the wire to fit the feeder.

Litterboxes. Start with at least two litterboxes. One is small, about 9x12″ for a single rabbit; 15x 18″ for two rabbits—for use inside the cage. The second and larger litterbox is to be used on the floor when you begin to let bunny have some free running time.

Litter. Nearly all pet supply stores now carry at least one rabbit-safe litter. Avoid clumping litters, dusty clays, and softwood bedding, such as pine or cedar.* There is no need to take health risks when there are so many safe organic litters to choose from—paper fiber, mountain grasses, wheat, corn cob, and citrus peel, to name a few.

Of course you don't want bunny to chew and swallow large amounts of any kind of litter. If you've purchased one that your bunny finds too tasty, then switch to another. Litters can cause internal damage and should not be ingested.

*Studies with other animals as far back as 1967 (Vesell 1967) show varying potential for respiratory disease and elevated liver enzymes.

"Plan on a limited area during the training and orientation period."

If organic litter is unavailable in your area, you can use a thick layer of straw on top of several layers of newspaper in a large tub or box.

Synthetic sheepskin rug. This adds comfort inside the cage and helps avoid some rabbits' tendency to sleep in their litterbox.

Containers. Large stackable plastic boxes are handy for storing pellets, hay, and litter.

Toys. These are more of a necessity than you might think. Add at least one chew toy and one nudge/toss toy (from chapter 3).

Instant starter space: All it takes is a baby gate at the door of a small room, such as the breakfast nook (right), where human family members can visit and bunny can have some freedom close to the litterbox. An indoor play yard (above) can be set up anywhere in the house. These are excellent training pens with a litterbox enclosed and a seagrass mat underneath.

STARTER SPACE

Even though you may plan on having bunny run and play throughout your entire house, this arrangement should evolve gradually. Plan on a limited area during the training and orientation period. Bathrooms, service porches, hallways, or kitchens can make ideal training rooms. Set this room up with the same furnishings as the cage, then add a few more items.

Baby gate. Instead of having a closed door between you and your bunny, invest in a baby gate, so that you can see her and talk to her.

Play yard. If you have a large open area that can't be sectioned off with baby gates, you can get an indoor play yard from a pet supply or toy store. These are wonderful training pens. They fold down and can be moved elsewhere or stored. You may pull it out of storage long after your bun has

free run of the house, perhaps when you get a second rabbit or bunny-sit for a friend.

Seagrass mats. These are good starter-space floor coverings to take toenail-and-tooth wear.

MORE-INVENTIVE HOUSING

With all the basics in place, you are ready to bring home your first house rabbit. When beginning life with a first rabbit, especially a baby rabbit, you may not be thinking of an elaborate habitat. You might in the future, however, want to go a step further and remodel your store-bought cage—add a second room or a second story, make a stand for it,

or incorporate it into an article of furniture. Once you have become well acquainted with your bunny, you will know which direction take.

The more popular housing styles that have developed in the past few years are multi-level condominiums with ramps or steps. The split-level Milwaukee condo on the left appeared in the last edition. Since then, my husband and I had the opportunity to meet its designer, Carolyn Long and see the habitat, ourselves. For the years of wear, it has held up surprisingly well, with only minor repair (of chewed wood strips). The L-shaped structure fits under a pottery/toy shelf. It has three removable doors, and the main "hall" is big enough for a human to sit in.

Two story condos with ramps between the floors (shown on page 46) have made a big hit in rabbit circles. Ramps have many uses. Elizabeth TeSelle's rabbits use a ramp in their cage-playground set up in their Nashville home (below).

The House Rabbit Society has received numerous ideas for habitats that range from very simple solutions to highly imaginative interactive living spaces. More information is available upon request if you send a self-addressed stamped envelope to HRS (address on page 94). ∎

TRAINING NATURALLY

Replace rules *with provisions: boxes of litter, comfortable bedding, and a vast array of toys. Your rabbit's positive behavior will be the natural outcome.*

Foster rabbit Jeffrey.
Helen Lau (inset) and Kappa

LET THE ENVIRONMENT DO THE WORK

YEARS OF FOSTERING RABBITS have taught us that rabbits are trained through their environment and their natural inclinations. All we have to do is make it easy for a new bunny of any age to do the "right" thing. Reprimands have no place in bunny training and, in fact, greatly interfere in establishing good habits in a natural way. The litterbox should be a wonderfully inviting place, never to be associated with punishment.

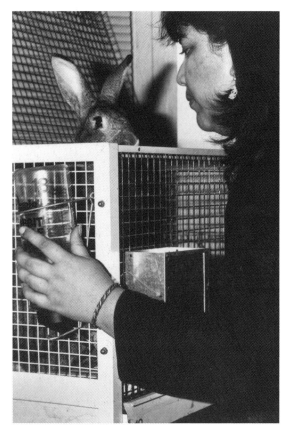

Also, the litterbox should be a convenient choice. Start in a small area.

BEGINNER TIME

Bunny's first day in your home should be spent primarily in the cage. I have "trained" rabbits from six weeks to six years all the same way. You may feel the task is hopeless at times, but take heart. It will be accomplished.

You run into your first snag: bunny sits in the comfortable litterbox all day and does her business out in the cage. This behavior can be averted by putting something equally comfortable, like a synthetic sheepskin rug, on the floor of the cage or in an additional box. For example, I have one little fellow who has impeccable habits now, but two years ago, he insisted on sleeping in his litterbox. I put a second box in his cage, so that one contained litter; the other, a rug. He chose to sleep on the soft rug and came to associate the litter with its appropriate use.

For the first few weeks, litterbox training should continue to take place mainly in the cage. Rabbits start using a litterbox because they like it. Each time they use it, they find it easier to use again. A habit is formed, as they train themselves.

When you add freedom, use the small starter space that you have sectioned off (page 19), so that bunny has access at all times to a local litterbox and can continue self-training. Set up the area in advance with at least one large litterbox in the corner. If more litterboxes are needed, add them. This will not last forever. The choices will eventually narrow down to a favorite place.

Cage time is learning time: Stacey can get acquainted with her litterbox, inside the cage, and get acquainted with Tania at the same time. Good habits can be firmly entrenched before bunnies have the freedom of the house.

PHOTOGRAPH: BOB HARRIMAN

"With a large hay tub, chewing and litterbox needs can be met in one package."

TERRITORIAL MARKING

Understand that rabbits need to mark new territory with urine or feces in order to feel that they belong in that environment. The litterbox can meet this need in their environment as something they can dutifully "mark." That's why you start with too many rather than too few litterboxes.

It is advisable to keep bunny off the beds and up-holstered furniture until after neutering and a litter-box habit is well established.

Exuberant bunnies may like to mark their play area immediately when they are let out of the cage. If you take them straight to a large litterbox from the cage, they soon get the idea that the litterbox is the territory to mark, and they associate it with their freedom. Within a few weeks, you can open the cage door, and they'll make a beeline for the litterbox on the floor.

FINDING DIRECTIONS

In addition to a large litterbox in new territory, plenty of "chewables" should be provided. House-training a rabbit means keeping both ends pointed in the right direction. With a large hay tub, chewing and litterbox needs can be met in one package. Don't worry about contamination. Rabbits eat from the corner opposite their "bathroom" corner. As your bunny matures and begins to take on full run of the house, his regular use of the litterbox should evolve naturally from

Convenient and inviting: *Bandit (upper) finds outlets for his natural urges (chewing and eliminating) in a large hay tub. The depth keeps most of the straw inside.*
Oscar (lower) finds a convenient litterbox during his first running time in his new play area.

PHOTOGRAPHS, UPPER: MARINELL HARRIMAN, LOWER: AMY ESPIE

23

"They are blessed with the ability to live, very much, in the present moment."

what he wants to do anyway.

If your bunny is not becoming self-trained, you may be giving too much space too soon. Or you may not be making the litterbox(es) enticing enough. Even a small litterbox can be made more inviting with a handful of hay in one corner. Make it something he can't resist.

Good toilet habits may take several weeks or months to achieve, depending on maturity. Don't expect a perfectly housetrained bunny at six weeks old.

Post-adolescent spayed or neutered rabbits are much less territorial and much more reliably house-trained. The notion that a mature rabbit is untrainable is nonsense! An ambulatory healthy older rabbit is more inclined to settle into a routine and is a very likely candidate for successful litterbox training. ∎

Learning from the Experts

AMY ESPIE

*W*E HUMANS ARE A TALKATIVE SPECIES. *Most of our communications are conducted through the written or spoken word. Sharing our lives with rabbits gives us the opportunity to learn a language based more on body position, facial expression and actions. Observation of rabbits conversing with one another provides lessons in grammar and vocabulary as well as in rabbit rules of etiquette.*

Rabbits have evolved an enviably simple, direct philosophy: If an experience, event, or behavior is pleasant and rewarding, pursue it; if unpleasant, stressful, or frightening, avoid it. Convoluted motivations such as spite or revenge are refreshingly absent. When a rabbit has a grievance, she's not shy to air it. When Daisy's partner gets between Daisy and a slice of banana, she immediately and clearly corrects him for this gaffe. She doesn't waste time sulking or plotting revenge when a simple, sudden, and well-aimed nip is so much more effective. With few lessons, Milo learns to place himself on the far side of the banana.

Daisy and Milo demonstrate two basic elements of training—timing and association. Rabbits know that in training, timing is all. At the exact instant when Daisy wants Oscar to get out of the way, she nips him.

This explains why a squirt of water in the face of rabbits who are fighting makes sense. It's short and sharp and immediately produces the desired response. Similarly, a handful of hay placed in one corner of the litterbox provides a perfectly timed reward for anyone who happens to hop in.

If the sight of her carrier always signals a trip to the vet, then we are using the power of association to (inadvertently) train Daisy to run and hide whenever she sees the carrier. If, on the other hand, the carrier is a place where she regularly finds a tasty treat and a welcoming rug, we are helping to minimize the stress of travel. In addition, since we know that stress contributes to illness, we can think of this as a health-maintenance exercise.

Of course rabbits have memory just as we do, but they also are blessed with the ability to live very much in the present moment. When they're angry, they fight. When they're happy, they grind their teeth. They don't harbor long-simmering grudges. If you're looking for role models in your effort to be here now, look no further. ∎

BUNNY-PROOFING

ONCURRENTLY WITH TRAINING HERSELF to use a litterbox, your rabbit will be training you to bunny-proof your house. Before allowing her full run of the house, survey the accessible areas. Her first running time should be carefully supervised. Have you moved all valuable books, magazines, and potted plants to higher shelves? Are all electrical cords covered up or out of reach? If you don't want bunny to chomp down on your computer cords, don't allow the cords to dangle into bunny's chewing range. Rabbits cannot resist nibbling on these long "vines." Is that chair pushed all the way under the desk when left unoccupied? If not, it can be used as a springboard by a whiskered explorer to access the desktop.

Your bunny-proofing efforts may require no more than picking up a few items. On the other hand, additional chewing temptations may be waiting to be discovered. Chances are you won't know how well your home is bunny-proofed until bunny has tested your handiwork.

REPELLENTS

If your bunny really has a mindset to chew on forbidden items, you may extend your repertoire of repellents, cover-ups, or diversions. Repellents are any of those odors that bunny finds repulsive. Some of these you may already have on your dresser—perfumes, shaving lotions, and various fragrances. Repellents from your garage are best not used in your house (e.g. carburetor cleaner, motor oil). Rejected men might believe that their rabbits show gender preference. Don't take it personally. Rabbits are not fond of men *or* women who have recently made automotive repairs.

Dog and cat repellents can be used, but don't over do it! Dense atomizing will keep bunny, and you too, completely away from the area. A tiny spray will do the job. Repellent sprays should be

Office experience: *An outstanding worker, Professor Tobias takes on the job of keyboarding in this Buffalo, New York home-office.*

reapplied daily until bunny has lost interest in the forbidden object.

Many people have experimented with tastes, applying bitters or red-pepper sauce. I find these inconsistent for keeping bunnies out of trouble. Turning them off with bad odors before they chomp down is safer.

COVER-UPS

Any of those things that hide or enclose the forbidden article, such as the phone cord, we call a cover-up. Numerous items can adequately serve this purpose, but you will want to use those that will not destroy your home decor at the same time. The ones that have worked for us without being too obtrusive are:

Plexiglas. A transparent hard-surface cover-up for linoleum or hardwood floors or lower wall areas.

PHOTOGRAPH: CHERYL O'CONNELL

Wooden bumpers. A thin strip of untreated wood can be tacked onto a baseboard. It protects the baseboard and provides a chewing border.

Polyethylene tubing. Tubing is sold by the foot in hardware stores and comes in a variety of diameters. With a sharp utility knife, slit it lengthwise and push the electrical cord inside.

Furniture arrangement. This is also a way to hide wiring. Block the access to electrical outlets with a piece of furniture. A disposable straw waste basket can be placed nearly anywhere.

Seagrass mats. These inexpensive, disposable organic rugs can be laid on top of more expensive rugs (that are harmful if chewed). This is a great diversion for cat clawing as well as bunny chewing.

Blanket throws/towels. For protection against toenails and teeth, these can be tossed over upholstery or beds. They take the day-to-day wear and fur accumulation.

We've learned, however, that rabbit chewing is not something to prevent but rather something to encourage. We should not expect and should not want our rabbits, no matter how domesticated, to entirely lose their natural urges to chew, dig, explore, and claim territory. It is our human responsibility to provide outlets for these needs. ■

PHOTOGRAPH: AMY ESPIE

DIVERSIONS FOR THE MENTALLY ACTIVE

A baleful or a mouthful: chewable toys divert bunnies' teeth from household furnishings to healthy recreation.

RABBITS ARE PROGRAMMED both mentally and physiologically to chew. Their bodies require it for nutritional and functional reasons. These needs are manifested in recreational chewing. Rabbits need indigestible organic fiber—but not synthetic fiber, such as your carpet. Give your rabbits such engaging things to chew that they won't even think about chewing the carpet.

POPULAR CHEW-TOYS

The top of the list in bunny chewables are *straw* and *wood* of all kinds. Straw can be given in a bale, in a bag, loose in a box, or woven into baskets or rugs. That large hay tub mentioned earlier takes on a new meaning as a bunny-proofing technique. A tub filled with straw will provide an abundance of chewing pleasure in a confined area, so that it won't be all over your carpet.

Disposable straw and wicker baskets come in many sizes and shapes. Bunnies love them all. Busy Bunny Baskets™, filled with edible toys, are available in many pet supply shops and are good examples of things you can give your rabbit.

Pet supply companies manufacture a variety of wooden toys for dogs and parrots. These are safe for rabbits to chew. Also, untreated scrap wood or firewood with bark, as well as small tree branches are good for chewing. Avoid redwood, which is toxic. Also, some fruit woods, such as cherry, peach, apricot, and plum are toxic, unless they have been dried for at least a month. The toxicity is present while the wood has sap. Since it may be hard to remember which freshly cut woods to avoid, you can simply age and dry all tree branches before bunny chews them.

MENTAL WORKOUTS

For both chewing satisfaction and mental workouts, rabbits are interested in a variety of toys. They are known to be quite imaginative with some of them. Although we use toy diver-

PHOTOGRAPHS: BOB HARRIMAN

"...we who live with house rabbits have known this all along."

sions to save our house, rabbits respond to them because they need mental stimulation. This idea was scoffed at a few short years ago. "Rabbits don't have the intelligence to play with toys," I was told by one scientist in a university lab.

In more recent years, "controlled" studies on cage enrichment confirm that rabbits do indeed interact with toys and with other animals whenever given the opportunity. (Brooks 1993) This proclamation by the scientific community has certainly improved the quality of life for some rabbits in laboratories, who are much less fortunate than our own, but of course we who live with house rabbits have known this all along.

What do rabbits respond to? Noisy (especially at 3:00 a.m.), jingly, rattly, bouncy things, such as mason-jar lids, wire balls, car keys, empty soup cans, and (non-breakable) hard plastic baby toys.

Toys for the mood: *Brit (left) selects a chewable branch while Barley (upper right) takes a mobile approach. Daphne (lower right) slings a noisy wire ball.*

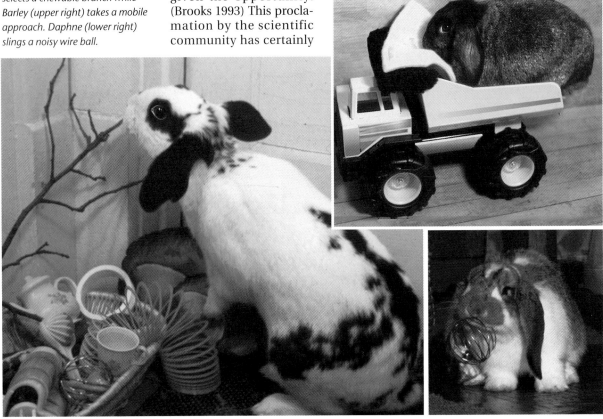

PHOTOGRAPHS, LEFT, UPPER RIGHT: CAROLYN LONG, LOWER RIGHT: MARINELL HARRIMAN

"Rabbits can do all kinds of things with a cardboard box."

On the quieter side, a towel on a slick floor gives bunny something to scoot around, bunch up, spread out, pat down, then roll up and scoot around again. Empty salt cartons and toilet paper spools can also be nudged and rolled on the floor.

Rabbits can do all kinds of things with a cardboard box. They can sit inside it, hop on top, chew it, scratch it, dig in it, and knock it about. Paper bags may serve a similar purpose. Can bunny chew too much cardboard? While it is possible for a rabbit to swallow excessive cardboard, it is not too likely. They can process a fair amount of indigestible fiber (without staples), and most of what they chew is left in shreds on the floor, anyway.

Toys are good for you. They save your house. And toys are good for your rabbit, who needs mental activity. Give your rabbit plenty of things to play with, and you will both be happy ■

PHOTOGRAPHS, UPPER: MARINELL HARRIMAN, LOWER: AMY ESPIE

AMUSEMENTS FOR MAYIM

A PHENOMENON WITNESSED by many rabbit watchers is an interactive game we call "chase the towel" or "ring around the towel." You can hold the towel and slowly spin around, dragging the towel over the bunny until she starts to chase it around your feet. Or you can fasten the towel to a chair. Many rabbits will circle it, tug on it, or just run through it, apparently enjoying the challenge.

In one city apartment, dangling scarves and piles of fabric are the objects of amusement. Mayim, a free-running rabbit, has tasted a few legal documents belonging to her human friend, Ezra Greenberg, a New York

Fabric fashions: Mayim studies the latest textile designs in her cage decor (upper) and on her favorite humans ,Ezra (middle) and Inci (lower).

lawyer. But nothing suits Mayim's fancy as much as her scarves. "She paws at them and bites them and just has a great time with them," Ezra tells us.

The cloth-toy idea originated with Ezra's friend, Inci Ali, who spent time watching Mayim's towel antics. "She often likes to scrunch up a towel and scratch the towel in a very aggressive manner with her paws," Inci observed.

Thinking of ways to extend the game, Inci remembered how, as a child, she built herself little tents with bedsheets. So she designed a bunny-style tent with hanging scarves for Mayim to play with. "She dives and squooshes into the scarves," says Inci, "and even growls at them."

Speaking seven languages herself, Inci was nonetheless surprised to discover Mayim's "rich and vibrant bunny vocabulary" and a panoply of growls, grunts, and squeals.

Whatever real-life situation the fabric game mimics is still a mystery. Whether the fabrics become a make-believe monster to conquer or a subordinate rabbit to bully, bunnies have a good time combating these fabricated creatures. ∎

NOTE: *Fabrics in a rabbit cage should be cut to short lengths that cannot entangle the rabbit. Remove any cloth that is excessively chewed.*

PHOTOGRAPHS: DON POLLARD

RAPPORT WITH HUMANS

Friendship with a rabbit comes with familiarity and by learning to think more like a rabbit. A family approach is an observation circle, in which humans can watch bunny and bunny can investigate humans.

Foster rabbits Ted and Lilac try out Bill and Amy Harriman's family—Nico, Aladdin, and Rian.

SOCIALIZING

I NO LONGER BELIEVE THAT RABBITS need to be socialized. They are all sociable. They interact with toys, with each other, and with other animals. People who live with rabbits in a household are eager to have these naturally sociable creatures interact with humans. How do you encourage this interactivity? Certainly not by sticking the rabbit off in a hutch, where he becomes bored and "boring." Include him in your daily life. Place a daytime cage, or set up a starter space, in an area where you spend a lot of time.

HEARING IS BELIEVING

You might assume that rabbits don't like to hear the phone ring. On the contrary, they accustom quickly to whatever buzzer, bleeper, or chime signals your phone calls. Then a wonderful thing happens—your voice. Even though rabbits do not often vocalize, they are soothed by a friendly human voice. The first way to socialize with a new bunny in your home is to have a lengthy phone conversation with a friend. Talk to, at, and around your bunny.

I discovered this several years ago after picking up five new rabbits from the animal shelter. There were cages waiting in the living room. I had other business to attend to and spent most of the afternoon on the phone, which was also in the living room. About two hours into the afternoon, I glanced around to find every one of the rabbits either stretched out in relaxation or rolled over in euphoria.

INTIMATE SPACE

Orientation to humans begins with a routine. If you are away at work all day, proximity is a must when you are home. Intimacy develops in a routine of proximity. This is unlikely to occur with an outdoor rabbit—unless you sleep outside, eat your meals there, and conduct your business from an outdoor phone. Getting close to your companion requires putting in the time. If you are a busy person, that's hard to do—unless your time serves double duty. You can do a lot of rou-

Fellowship of the Floor: *Some of the best things happen in low places. Nim gives affection-nuzzles to her human, Charlie.*

PHOTOGRAPH: AMY ESPIE

Cozy methods: *Pepper and Kay Leiker of Wichita sit lap style (upper), while Stacey prefers the next-to position (lower).*

tine tasks while socializing with your rabbit in a small area, maybe just one room. Although bunny needs a few safe hideaways, these should not be so remote that she disappears and you never see each other. Just as in house-training, have the environment work *for* you.

Have social sessions in which you meet her at her level. Put yourself in her running space and wait. There is no need to rush her. You don't need to grab, hold, restrain, or coax her into your lap. We tell this to children often, and it is one of the most important things for a human of any age to know about their bunnies. Rabbits sit close to each other. To socialize with you, let bunny initiate it—usually on the floor, but a bed may work, too. Occupy the same space, then do homework, read a book, or watch TV. She will come to you, because she can't help it. It's in her nature. She will investigate you as she does all objects in her environment.

HAND WORKS

Hands are not always the best means to earn a rabbit's trust. Even small children find that a better way to communicate is the way a rabbit does—nose to nose. Although rabbits best understand face-to-face intimacy, humans more often use their hands to express affection to an animal.

Rabbits, however, may misinterpret their

meaning. Is the approaching hand a threat or a giver of rewards? You must make your intentions clear. When stroking a rabbit for the first time, approach directly from the top of the head, not under the chin. Since hands can be visually frightening, let her *feel* the stroke of your hand on her head and down her back before attempting the lower parts of the face. Rabbits groom each other around the eyes, top of the nose, top of the head, ears, and down the back. Stroking them in these areas is more readily understood as friendly.

As bunny comes to enjoy the feeling of being stroked, you may push the intimacy further with

PHOTOGRAPHS, UPPER: TANIA HARRIMAN, LOWER: MARINELL HARRIMAN

"...you'll be glad something is between you and the toenails trying to get a foothold."

a flea comb. We use a flea comb as much for socialization as we do for actually catching fleas. Somehow, bunnies sense our good intentions, and we have used a flea comb to mellow out some of our most aloof rabbits.

Again, start high on the head and don't come around to the under side of the face until after several weeks of combing/brushing higher on the head. Soon, you will have a bunny begging you for a flea combing.

LAP SITTING

Your rabbit may not want to sit entrapped on your lap. As you sit on the floor, she will nudge and sniff and maybe hop onto your lap momentarily. A towel spread across your lap will make it more inviting to your bunny, and you will be glad something is between you and the toenails that are trying to get a foothold. Let her hop on and off your lap at will.

When handling rabbits, protect yourself with a barrier of clothing! Don't blame your bunny for trying to get a more secure toenail grip. Scratching has nothing to do with malice but rather with balance and footing.

Declawing a rabbit is *not* the solution. Instead keep the toenails clipped short, learn appropriate handling, and don't expose bare skin.

Small children should not be allowed not pick up rabbits at all. The best way children *and adults* can learn about rabbits is from the ground up. ∎

Deeply felt experience: *Don Wild of San Francisco,(above) who lives with multiple rabbits, pays with a pound of flesh for taking the toenail risk.*
Summer-wear offers little protection when bunny is climbing on a human lap. Amy Harriman takes a precautionary measure (left). A towel should be spread across all bare laps before exposure.

PHOTOGRAPHS, LEFT: MARINELL HARRIMAN, RIGHT: JANIS WILD

FROM AGGRESSION TO AFFECTION

ONE PART OF BUNNY VOCABULARY that people most often misinterpret is biting. By observing "rabbit rules of etiquette" (described on page 24) and by understanding the occasions in which bunny uses "bite-words," you can avoid having these conversations. Here are a few of the occasions and ways to circumvent them.

Testing. It's common for baby rabbits to go through a period of testing their teeth. If your bunny decides to test his teeth on you, I advise a small screech. This is a sound rabbits make in dire distress. He will understand that this is serious business.

Move over. Rabbits may nip whatever is in their way. It can be another rabbit who is blocking the water bottle or a human arm that is confining a rabbit to a lap. Screeching may work, but it might be better to avoid using part of your body as a barricade.

Zealous grooming. When grooming each other, rabbits pull out burrs and chew foreign particles entangled in each other's fur. Keep this in mind when your rabbit friend is licking your sleeve or pant leg and comes to a seam or wrinkle that could be interpreted as removable.

Defense. As stated earlier, objects coming from below eye level may appear threatening. Don't stick your hand up to a rabbit's nose to be sniffed as you would to a dog or scratch under the chin as you would a cat. Your extremities, hands or feet, may be judged separately from the rest of yourself, so don't assume that your bunny doesn't like you if he distrusts your hands. It may take a while to connect those foreign objects to you.

Side approach. A human hand is all the more threatening to a shy rabbit when it is reaching in through a small side-opening cage door. As you invade her "safe" haven, she backs into the far corner, forcing you to approach her from the front at eye level. You must find a way to approach from the top, even if it means installing a new top-opening door or enlarging the one on the side.

Aromatic fingers. If you have been eating pretzels or dicing carrots, don't stick your fingers into bunny's cage.

Possessiveness. Unspayed females and many unneutered males may be particularly protective of their possessions, and it's best to clean the cage when it is unoccupied.

Misdirection. A human referee may incur a misdirected bite for trying to intervene between two rabbit adversaries—in much the same way that a person gets scratched by grabbing a cat from an attacking dog. You might also receive a misdirected bite if you carry the scent of a "foreign" rabbit on your clothing.

I have to comment on rabbits labeled "biters." The best way to "cure" aggression in a rabbit is to redirect the energy by meeting animosity with benevolence. When aggression is channeled into affection, the bite becomes a lick. Some of my most affectionate rabbits are converted biters.

For instance, every time we walked into his room, our rabbit Bandit would come lunging and growling to bite our ankles, only to find himself getting a thorough rub-down, brushing, flea combing, or scratches behind the ears. His lunges soon became exuberant greetings accompanied by a silly dance.

The assertive rabbit may always need to assert. But when the urge to attack is combined with a fondness for the attacked, the bite attack is replaced by an affection attack, just as gratifying as having a dog meet you at the door. It's well worth your effort to establish a loving relationship with an aggressive-affectionate rabbit. ■

FRIENDLY LIFTOFFS

YOU WILL PROBABLY DISCOVER that bunny doesn't particularly like to be picked up and carried around. He may enjoy cozying up beside you, but being lifted and carried is a different matter. However, there are times when you *must* pick up your rabbit—to remove him from danger or take him to the veterinarian.

For this reason I recommend a daily exercise in lifting and handling. Pick him up and set him down again. A brief, non-stressful lift followed by a small reward will help a rabbit overcome the fear of being lifted. Our formerly reluctant Phoebe caught on quickly. She soon began to circle my feet, tripping me, if I forgot her treat when I set her down.

Our foster rabbits must be carried frequently, and trial-and-error has provided lifting techniques that work for most. Two positions that I use are shoulder-rump and feet-to-chest. I lift all larger rabbits by the shoulders and rump.

Side-door approach: *The trick is to lift bunny's shoulders while scooping the hindquarters towards you.*

PHOTOGRAPH: AMY ESPIE

"Caution must be used in setting bunny back down."

BIG BUNNY LIFT

To pick up a large rabbit from the floor, walk up confidently, get behind him, put one hand under the chest and one under the rump and lift—with authority. Don't act timid. My technique is to hold the hindquarters firm and low to prevent kicking. My veterinarian does it just the opposite, with the bunny rolled into a ball. Either way seems to prevent the feet from getting into kicking position. Rabbits have fragile skeletons. When the hind legs are suspended, a sudden kick could result in a broken back.

Caution must be used in setting bunny back down. This is a time when they often leap in anticipation. If you feel your bunny kicking out of your arms, drop into a squat on the floor. Reducing the height will reduce the chances of injury to your bunny or yourself.

SMALL BUNNY LIFT

Smaller rabbits are usually better picked up from the front. They tend to feel more secure with their front feet resting on your collar bone or braced against your body for support. Place one hand under the forelegs and one hand under the rump and bring towards your body.

This lifting method is often the one that works best for children, since they are better able to use their whole body for support of the bunny. (Children should be over 8 years old.)

UP AND OUT

Rabbits can be lifted from a top-opening cage the same way as from the floor. Top-opening doors are much easier for you than side-opening doors. The hardest lifting situation that you can possibly attempt is to pull a rabbit, of any size, through a small side-opening door. To get bunny out, reach in and place your hands on top of his head, stroke him from head to tail, then scoop him toward you. Get your body close enough for him to get a footing with his front paws. This will make him secure enough to be pulled out the rest of the way. ∎

Rear support is important with all lifts. Big bunny lift (left) is from the back side. Little bunnies are more secure facing you (middle, right).

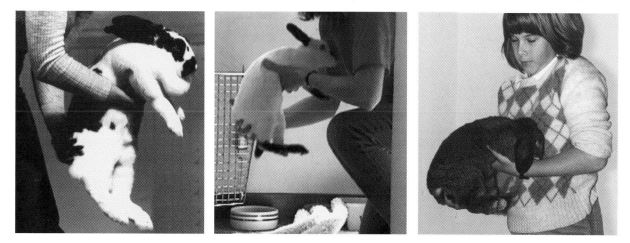

PHOTOGRAPHS, LEFT: BOB HARRIMAN, MIDDLE, RIGHT: MARINELL HARRIMAN

"Your child will learn most by watching you..."

Teaching Children to be Rabbit People

CAROLYN MIXON

WHEN LIVING WITH A RABBIT and children, there are two important concepts to accept. First, that the rabbit is your responsibility. Let your child help with the rabbit, but don't insist. Your child will learn most by watching you— your actions, attitude, and tone of voice. Secondly, remember that many rabbits are apprehensive towards children. Let the rabbit decide what kind of relationship he wishes to have with the children.

Whether you bring a rabbit home to your child's house or bring a baby home to your rabbit's house, you as the adult need to:

■ Learn about rabbit behavior/language so you can point out the rabbit's feelings about your child's actions.

■ Anticipate and prevent inappropriate behavior by setting up situations for success. This helps to:

Art of Love: Emily Mixon of Austin, Texas refines her petting skills with Jessie rabbit.

■ Avoid having to reprimand your child for bothering the rabbit. Be generous with praise when the child is gentle with and respectful of the rabbit.

The most effective reprimand is to keep the child away from the rabbit for a short time. Repeated or frequent misbehavior means the child is not ready for a relationship with the rabbit. Wait until the child is older before trying to reintroduce them.

■ Set up the cage so the rabbit can get away from children. Use child gates and/or turn the cage so that the door faces a wall with enough room for a rabbit but not a child.

■ Put the rabbit in a closed-off room when there are lots of young guests.

■ Show children's friends where the rabbit lives and how to pet, only when 1 or 2 friends visit. Never leave children unsupervised with the bunny.

■ Establish and actively teach these Bunny Rules:

1. Gentle Petting: Teach slow, gentle strokes on the head, ears, and upper back, using two fingers or back of hand to prevent fur-grabbing or eye-pokes.

2. Follow Bunny's Lead: Teach respect for the rabbit by allowing him to be the one to start and end a visit. Leave the rabbit alone when he hops into his cage. Supervise and prevent children from chasing or poking at the rabbit through the cage. Interpret rabbit's body language for the child. ("He doesn't want any more petting. He wants to rest.")

3. On Friendly Ground: Explain that "it scares the rabbit to be picked up, and both of you could get hurt." Explain that an adult may pick up the rabbit if he needs care.

Children learn nurturing and joyful appreciation from you, the responsible adult.   ■

NOTE: For more information on children and rabbits contact a local Humane Society, SPCA, or House Rabbit Society.

PHOTOGRAPH: CAROLYN MIXON

A RABBIT NAMED DOROTHY

DOROTHY WAS OVER two years old when she was adopted from our foster home. She lived out her life, another seven years, with a family that has become our model for structuring a rabbit-with-children environment. Dorothy's story, which appeared in the previous edition and also in the *House Rabbit Journal*, continues to set the standard for a successful arrangement of rabbits and children.

It was unlikely back in 1987 that I would let one of my most loved rabbits go into a home with a toddler and a three-year old child. From the time this wonderful 10-pound lop first arrived in our foster home, we wanted to keep her. I wasn't even planning to show her to Amy Berg and Hugh Douglas when they arrived with their two little boys. We had already turned down several would-be adopters, but the commitment Amy and Hugh demonstrated to teaching their children loving kindness and caring made us change our minds.

Sharing snacks and moments of contentment, three-year-old Will indulges an eager Dorothy in treats she deserves.

It was a perfect match for big, easy-going, affectionate Dorothy. Her size, Amy says, was an advantage against excited little hands. Before bringing Dorothy home they explained to three-year-old Will that they would all be taking care of the rabbit and that his special job was to be gentle and careful.

As Dorothy settled in, she developed a friendship with each family member, beginning with Hugh, dancing around his feet every morning and sitting on the couch next to him in the evening.

Her routine with Amy, during morning coffee-making, was to tug on Amy's robe or softly paw her legs until Amy stooped down to pet her.

Dorothy could often be found lying next to Will on the floor. He enjoyed getting her food, and the baby, Ethan, enjoyed giving Dorothy her daily allotment of crackers. There were times when a contented Dorothy could be seen between the two boys with each resting an arm across her.

Hearing these stories was gratifying for us, but we knew it was unrealistic to assume that young children growing up would never need a reminder to play gently with a live animal. Amy and Hugh were vigilant. If the play got too rough, the boys were restricted from playing with Dorothy. Hugh and Amy set a continuous example. "The foremost responsibility to make sure she is handled properly is mine and my husband's," said Amy.

Both boys learned to give Dorothy respect, love, and careful attention. Her willingness to sit close beside them and be caressed was their ongoing reward.   ■

Learning to Love Again

AMY BERG

SOMEHOW I KNEW IT WOULD TAKE two rabbits to roam the rooms that Dorothy left behind when she died. Of course I knew I'd never be able to "replace" her, any more than one can ever replace a beloved individual of any species. She was sweet and patient, and being our first house rabbit, Dorothy defined bunny love.

At night, after putting the kids to bed, I'd lie on the rug with Dorothy. She'd lick my face, soothing away the day's tensions. Sometimes my husband and I would find ourselves in the kitchen with all the animals: Rosie, the dog, Jeff and Al, the cats, and Dorothy. Rosie would groom Jeff while Al pounced on her tail, and Dorothy calmly watched the antics.

Dorothy asked for nothing and gave us her all. She even befriended the dog, whose arrival had changed her life, restricting her previously unlimited freedom. She patiently awaited her turn for attention, and she was often relegated to the end of the line because she didn't whine or meow or drop soggy rawhide bones on our laps.

We took Dorothy's death hard. Then we discovered that even in her death she gave to us. We shared our memories of her and that gave us strength. She taught us that healing comes out of the grieving process, but we had to be patient, as she had been.

I wasn't sure when I'd be ready to adopt a new rabbit, but when I got a call from the same shelter from which the House Rabbit Society had rescued Dorothy seven years earlier, the knowledge that it was right to bring home two rabbits rose from a place within me.

My sons had already chosen the names Tasha and Alex by the time the rabbits were ready to move into our house. They did not come to us accustomed to people, as Dorothy had. Becoming acquainted was a reciprocal process.

They are still a little shy and pull back until they're stroked. I love to watch their garden antics: Alex jumping straight into the air; Tasha hurdling flower beds. Sometimes they collide when I approach. I find their seemingly disgruntled attitude toward me humorous when, in the next moment, they can't get close enough if I'm bearing treats.

I welcome the differences. After all, they will never be Dorothy. The place she left behind in all of us is a place of love, healed now with the knowledge that the more one loves, the more love there is. Loving Dorothy opened our hearts all the more. I guess that's why I suspected it would take two rabbits to join her where she will always reside—in our family's collective hearts.   ■

PHOTOGRAPH, OPPOSITE PAGE: AMY ESPIE

Rabbits need friends. *Adding a companion or two can enhance your rabbit's life without diminishing friendship with you. Remember that rabbits live naturally in groups and are capable of multiple friends.*

Fiona (left), adopted companion for Downey. Franklin Chow (inset) with Kappa, Beta, and Lambda.

WHEN RABBITS MEET

SCIENTIFIC STUDIES BY VETERINARIANS at UC Davis (Brooks 1993) and other academic institutions have validated our long-held premise that rabbits are extremely sociable—so much so, that our House Rabbit Society fosterers don't even adopt to homes where the rabbit will live in solitude (e.g. a backyard hutch).

Although they are naturally sociable, rabbits don't always know this important fact about themselves. Or maybe they have forgotten it through the process of being "domesticated" and living in isolated quarters. When rabbits live with other rabbits, neutering is essential. While spayed/neutered rabbits may be considered less "natural," spayed/neutered rabbits, in actuality, are able to enjoy a more natural lifestyle, since they can run about freely together and work out social structures.

When given a choice rabbits live naturally in groups, yet some are much more monogamous than others, and living as bonded pairs is more natural for them. The easiest introduction is between a neutered male and a spayed female. However, after several successes in introducing companions of the same sex, I am much more optimistic about this possibility than I used to be.

RABBIT SEXUAL PSYCHOLOGY

We start with rabbits who are neutered or spayed. Contrary to logical assumption, rabbit sexual activity does not necessarily end with sterilization, and newly introduced rabbits often engage in a passionate courtship (which is preferable to a combative relationship). Rabbit sexuality is largely a mental attitude.

Why should the female be spayed if the male is neutered? Aside from all the health reasons to

PHOTOGRAPH: AMY ESPIE

First Date: *Suitable neutral territory for the introduction of this neutered pair is a Madison, Wisconsin bathtub.*

be discussed in chapter 7, this is the scenario. She will be mounted by the neutered male for the first day. Then suddenly her mood changes as she enters a false pregnancy. She rejects his advances and busies herself with destructive (to your house) activities, shredding paper and maybe curtains to build her nest. Meanwhile, he can't understand why she has a continuous "headache." She won't be receptive to his amorous advances for another month. Neutered pairs have a lot more fun than that.

Sometimes a rabbit mounts another backwards. This may be part of the seductive foreplay, but it can be quite risky for the rabbit on top if the rabbit underneath is uncooperative. I'm sure that veterinarians who repair the damage consider it malicious intent by one rabbit to amputate the genitals of another. (More likely it is a defensive act by the rabbit on the bottom.) When you see backwards mounting, always intervene to protect the top bunny.

GETTING PREPARED

Since the previous edition, I've standardized my techniques for introducing rabbits to each other. I make two assumptions. Yes, the rabbits will hate each other at first sight and, yes, they will become bonded friends. The second assumption for me is a matter of experience. For a beginner it's a matter of faith. Admittedly, there are times during the introduction process that I, too, would give up if I didn't know better.

The advice I give is to prepare for the worst, and if you have an easier time, so much the better. The materials you will need are two cages, a water bottle with a spray pump, and some neutral territory (not part of either rabbit's normal environment). The territory should be large enough to allow a little distance between the rabbits but not so large that they forget each other's existence. A bathroom, a service porch, or playpen would be ideal—not much larger than 10 x 12, or smaller than a standard bathtub.

INTRODUCTORY STEPS

These are typical procedures. Variations depend on your particular space and "props."

Week 1: Cages side-by-side. Put the rabbits in the two cages at night. Exercise them in separate areas during the day.

Week 2: Daily car rides. Leave the bunnies loose in the back seat with maybe a litterbox on the seat. They won't fight while the engine is running. After 20 minutes of driving around in traffic, you should find them huddled together in the litterbox.

If the entire back seat of your car seems too big to bring them together, section off a smaller space that will keep them close.

Separate them again when you take them back into the house, but keep their cages side-by-side.

"...it won't be long, maybe a day or two, before they are grooming each other."

Signs of acceptance: *When either rabbit assumes a "presentation smile" (above), it means they will be able to work things out. When one grooms the other (right), an amicable relationship exists.*

Week 3: Continued daily car rides. Leave bunnies together for about 5 minutes after you turn off the ignition. If they fight, separate them sooner; if not, you can give them a few extra minutes.

Week 4. Small neutral territory. Give the bunnies 20 minutes a day, gradually increasing the time. Begin the week with a car ride, but instead of separating them afterwards take them to the neutral space—but first, note their attitude. Are they quiet or energetic? If either rabbit is quiet, you can skip the following step. If they are energetic and you feel a lot of tension, get into their space with the spray bottle and supervise them. Keep within spraying distance at all times, and if you see one rabbit start to attack the other, let him have it right in the face. He/she will take time out from the hostilities to face wash.

This triggers another interesting behavior in the acceptance process. (I know this from video-taping many introductions.) When you see newly introduced rabbits simply occupying the same territory, ignoring each other, but nervously grooming themselves, you can bet that it won't be long, maybe a day or two, before they are grooming each other. If the intended couple is not highly charged to begin with, you won't need to use the water bottle. Just supervise the rabbits for the first couple of days in their neutral territory for about 20 minutes, then gradually increase their time together.

The whole process usually takes about 5 weeks. You will notice them sitting on opposite sides of the territory. Gradually you will see them sitting closer together, then snuggling together during the day. Give them a few more days to firmly establish this cordial habit, then they are ready to share a bed and can remain together at night.

If you don't have a car to use for the first transition, you will have to start with neutral territory at week 2, but keep the time very short—5 minutes a day to begin with. Complete the rest of the process, gradually increasing their time together.

WHY GRADUAL?

Although friendship supports longevity in rabbits, introductions can be stressful to the immune system. Falling in love is one of life's most joyous experiences. But could anyone stand those butterflies in the stomach forever? Fortunately most creatures settle into a comfortable relationship in time. When rabbits are first intro-

"...house-trained residents assist with litterbox lessons."

duced, the "butterfly" period sometimes results in loose bowels. And in their excitement, most "honeymooners" temporarily forsake their good toilet habits, so you will have some extra cleanup for a couple of days.

Whenever we introduce older, chronically ill, or in any way compromised animals, we use extreme caution—in much the same way that gradual dietary changes are made—little bit at a time. Why introduce them at all? The potential for a positive and mutually beneficial relationship, if done gradually, outweighs the risk. The reason I proceed slowly in introducing *all* rabbits is to keep from over-taxing any immune system that might be fighting a subclinical disease in a seemingly healthy rabbit.

RABBITS IN GROUPS

Putting together a group of rabbits is usually easier than introducing two individuals at a time. This may be due to a natural tendency of rabbits to fall into a hierarchical structure. Group introductions, up to about seven rabbits, can be handled generally the same way as for singles. With very large groups, it's not always possible to find neutral territory that hasn't already been claimed by one or two of the resident rabbits.

Rabbit rescuers who work with large group housing generally don't worry about neutral territory, but they do provide a larger space for the introduction, such as an entire backyard. They have a water hose ready, in case of serious fighting, but generally they rely on the rabbits' innate ability to structure a hierarchy.

When additional rabbits are introduced, the house-trained residents assist with litterbox lessons. I give very little thought to house-training when I introduce a new rabbit. After the "honeymoon" period, they learn from their mates. ∎

"...they choose to bed down with their friends in tight piles..."

How Rabbits Use Space

MARGO DE MELLO

URBAN PLANNERS KNOW that if people are given their own private space to claim, they will tend to behave in a territorial fashion within it, defending the boundaries of that space with fervor (as the new gated communities in Los Angeles show). And so it is with rabbits, another social species that sometimes seems to spend more time fighting with their own kind than living in harmony. In wild rabbits, territorial behavior includes depositing marking pellets at the boundaries of the territory, chinning, urinating, and aggressive behavior such as digging, circling and fighting. Wild males tend to defend larger territories while females concentrate on their nests. In our neutered and spayed domestic companions, the hormonal basis for much of this behavior disappears, but our rabbits continue to be affected by the constraints of space.

It seems obvious that when rabbits are confined to too small a space, their health and happiness will be compromised. Yet when my group of 24 foster rabbits sleep at night, they choose to bed down with their friends in tight piles on the top floors of their condos. While there's plenty of room on the bottom floor, the top floor provides them with a view, toys, and a carpet to lie on. In addition, they enjoy the close bodily comfort that they get from lying 5 or 6 to a cage.

When I recently switched from single rabbit cages to jumbo two-story condos, I witnessed a number of changes in the social composition of the group. Originally, the cages were grouped according to the social cliques that had developed, with the dominant group all sharing a number of joined cages, and the less dominant buns forming other social groups, large and small, throughout their room. When the first new cage arrived, however, the rabbits were so intrigued by it that many abandoned their former homes to crowd into this new environment. Territorial behavior seemed to diminish in light of the exciting new space, with its ramp, carpeted top floor, and window view.

Now that everyone has access to one of the new condos, the groups have shifted slightly, as preference for condo space sometimes overrides traditional friendships and old antagonisms. They are still territorial, however. While everyone knows (at least nominally) how to use a litterbox, most will still mark the doors to their cages. As always, the girls remain most aggressive towards newcomers, but as long as sleeping space shifts from night to night, territorial aggression is held at bay. Neutral space, in other words outside the cage, can be shared by all the rabbits. I expect that if they again choose definite places to sleep at night, they will again become more fervent in defending those spaces. ∎

Margo DeMello holds a PhD in cultural anthropology from University of California, Davis .

PHOTOGRAPH: MARINELL HARRIMAN

WHEN CATS AND RABBITS CO-EXIST

AS MUCH AS WE ENCOURAGE COMPANIONSHIP for all rabbits, this is not necessarily with each other. In some situations, the demands of their own society can be too stressful for certain rabbits to live happily. These animals often relate better to companions of another species. This is sometimes true of cats as well as rabbits. I've had cats who detest each other but adore the rabbits.

I am taken by surprise when someone calls who has just found a rabbit and says, "I can't keep it. I have a cat." The second statement has nothing to do with the first. A projection of my own statistics from incoming mail is that well over half of all rabbit people also have cats.

Cats and rabbits do not need to bed down together (although many of them do) in order to relate. Our first rabbit, Herman, and our cat, Nice, seldom touched, but they interacted in chase games—in and out of paper bags. A game of one-upsmanship occurred daily between the two. After being ambushed from behind the door, Herman waited until nap time to throw herself on top of the peacefully dozing cat.

Phoebe, Herman's successor, developed intimate rapport with Octavia. This was the kind of relationship that meant that when Phoebe was sick and needed around-the-clock care, Octavia stayed by her side for a full 48 hours—until the

Peaceful and playful: *Contact by mutual agreement (upper) or by a pushy cat (lower left) or a pushy rabbit (lower right).*

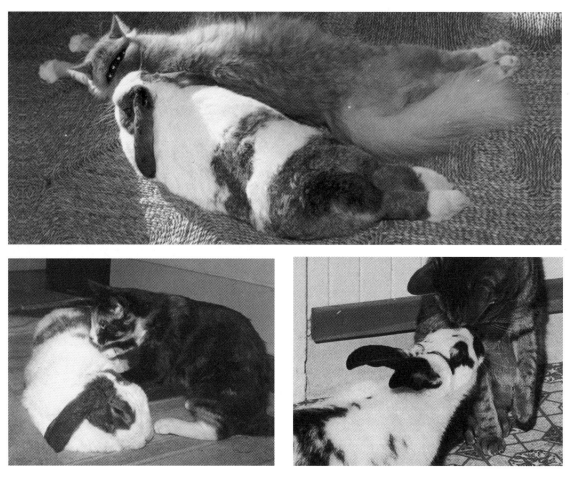

crisis passed. We believe that Octavia saved Phoebe's life.

Introductions during feisty adolescence of either species should be more carefully supervised. A lively, boisterous teenage cat can put dangerous claws into an unsuspecting bunny. And, of course, you should avoid introducing a very young bunny (rat-size) to a full-grown cat. On the other hand, big rabbits can bully a lighter weight cat, so equal size usually makes a better match.

Cats *and* rabbits of all ages should have their nails trimmed very short.   ■

PHOTOGRAPHS, UPPER, LOWER LEFT: AMY ESPIE, LOWER RIGHT: MARINELL HARRIMAN

HOW DOGS BECOME DOCILE WITH RABBITS

PHOTOGRAPH: AMY ESPIE

SUCCESSFUL RABBIT-DOG INTRODUCTIONS are large-ly dependent on the behavior of the dog, and it's absolutely crucial that the dog not chase if the rabbit runs. Because a single mishap can mean disaster, a relationship between a dog and a rabbit requires much more consideration, plan-ning, and supervision. I was not completely aware of this sequence at the time of our first experience. I came home from work one day to find my then 15-year-old son, Bill, with his dog, Rags, and our rabbit, Herman, sitting on the bedroom floor do-ing "homework." Looking back, I realize that all of

"They could sniff noses and get acquainted through the safety of the wire cage."

Inquisitive and cautious: With the strange new creature inside the puppy pen, Teddy gets his first close-up view of Xena.

the factors for success were already in place. Rags was mature, easy-going, and reliably obedience-trained She had a thorough understanding of the words "down-stay," "gentle," and "off." Based on my single experience with one dog, I assumed that mature dogs were the best candidates for companionship with rabbits.

Fourteen years later, we brought home a 7-month-old pup to our rabbits' house. I called on dog-trainer animal-behaviorist Amy Espie for help. In her e-mail reply from Virginia, she said, "You just want your pup to understand that the rabbits are family members, not prey. If Xena gets over-excited too much, there's no disadvantage to waiting a few months or weeks till she's older, calmer, or more used to the rest of her new surroundings before you try again with rabbits."

Amy went on to tell me how her "vicious" pit bull grooms her rabbits. Looking at my energetic

Xena, I couldn't imagine being able to trust her to that extent. Amy is a dog trainer, I thought. She can work magic with dogs.

INITIAL BEDLAM

I'm sure I am not the only person to bring home a new animal and think within the first hour, What have I done? When we brought Xena in the door, all the rabbits in our house started thumping in frenzy. Teddy and Lilac scurried out of the living room, and our cat, Octavia, bowed up her back and hissed and growled. The first evening looked like nothing was going to work. The very scent of a dog in the house, even in a distant room made all the rabbits very uneasy. The first task was just to get them accustomed to her presence in the house.

We opted for a 4 x 4' puppy pen to provide Xena with a place where she could be observed as unthreatening to the rabbits. We set up the pen in the same fashion as our rabbit cages—food and water dishes, bed, and toys. But without a litterbox, of course, it meant that we would take her out on a harness and leash several times a day. By the next morning things had calmed down. The cat was sitting on the coffee table next to Xena where she watched with curiosity.

We felt more optimistic about our prospects and began to videotape what we were certain would be the animals' progress. The next few weeks were managed in the following steps:

1. Rotated use of the yard. Xena used the backyard before the rabbits went out in the morning and after they came in at night. (We walked her on leash at other times).

2. A puppy pen part of the day. Curious rabbits could observe a dog who was contained in a pen. Free-running rabbits could be observed by the dog in a non-chase environment.

VIDEOGRAPH: MARINELL HARRIMAN

"The responsibility for their safety is with the people who live with them."

3. Supervised (leashed) time outside the pen.

4. Unleased time outside the pen when the rabbits were in their cages.

The rabbits gradually became accustomed to the noises and strange movements of the dog. They could sniff noses and get acquainted through the safety of the wire cage.

5. Dog-style exercise (with us)—running, jumping, fetching a ball, so that Xena would not need to play rough with the rabbits.

6. Participation in duties. Xena began to make the rounds with us as we gave nightly feedings. Her first real introduction was to a crippled rabbit who lives on our service porch. As I talked gently to Rousseau, filled his dish, and stroked him, Xena mimicked my manner with gentle grooming.

Now, whenever I brush or flea comb a rabbit, that's Xena's cue to wash the animal.

7. Commingling in our presence. We took down the puppy pen and allowed Xena freedom of the house. Not wanting to risk a sudden overwhelming impulse of a young playful pup, we never left her alone with the rabbits unless they were caged.

As she spent more and more time freely commingling with rabbits in our presence, we began to leave them together for short periods during their quiet times of day (afternoons).

8. Reward without reprimand. Xena's experience with the rabbits has always been positive. Amy had advised us to avoid situations that required reprimand—so that the rabbits were not a source of frustration. This is a fundamental concept in training any animal living in a human environment. It's called "setting up for success."

Although dog-and-cat playtime does include some two-way chase games, Xena's conduct with the rabbits is completely quiet and includes no rough play at all.

After a total of six unhurried months, we now have free-running rabbits living with a young dog, who requires no supervision with the rabbits and can be left alone with them for an indeterminate period of time.

Wanda meets "the boys" *Amy Espie's pitbull is anything but vicious. Effort taken for working through dog-training with the rabbit is well rewarded.*

BRINGING A RABBIT TO A DOG'S HOME

If you are bringing home a rabbit to your resident o*bedience-trained* dog, have a secure cage set up for the rabbit. The same precautions and steps already outlined are appropriate for a resident dog except that you will probably forego the puppy pen. Supervision is required along with judgement on your part as to when/if your dog and rabbit are ready to commingle.

Animals are what they are. The responsibility for their safety is with the people who live with them. If you trust your animals' behavior when supervised but not in your absence, that's no worse than in other kinds of parenting. You don't leave your human children unsupervised. ∎

PHOTOGRAPH: AMY ESPIE

HOW RABBITS AND GUINEA PIGS KEEP HOUSE

ANY ADDITIONAL INTEREST in the environment is better than loneliness and boredom. Interaction with smaller animals, such as hamsters, mice, and sometimes birds, will vary with the individuals. Rabbits and guinea pigs usually fall into easy friendships. Some guinea pigs boss rabbits around. One might grab a piece of apple from a very pushy rabbit, and the rabbit lets it happen.

Many rabbit rescuers have picked up guinea pigs among the rescues. I have. How could I go to an animal shelter and remove the two rabbits and leave that one small kennel mate behind? I have to say that clinically speaking, rabbits and guinea pigs are not supposed to be housed together. Practically speaking, we (rabbit rescuers) do it anyway. The danger is that some bacteria that are harmless in one species may cause trouble in another.

For instance, bacteria, such as Pasteurella, do not bother cats but can cause serious infections in rabbits. Other bacteria, such as Bordetella, may cause only minor or subclinical problems in rab-

bits and major disease in guinea pigs. For this reason, guinea books advise against caging colonies of rabbits and guinea pigs together.

Again, our practical experience shows mixed species happily sharing environments and living long lives. If you are putting together household companions and live in reasonable cleanliness, the risk appears to be minimal. If you are going into an animal production business, you will need to get a different book.

SHARED PLAYGROUNDS

Some people enjoy building guinea pigs elaborate habitats as they do for their rabbits. Sometimes a fenced-in playground is provided that the pigs and bunnies can share. The fence or wall can be as low as 1-foot high if you want your rabbits, but not your guinea pigs, to have access to the rest of the house.

If you let your guinea pigs have part-time run of the house, put a lot of little flat trays along the edges of the room. Another place they may designate as a "bathroom" is under the bed. We discovered this one time as we pulled out a flat storage box and found it had been converted to guinea pig litterbox.

Guinea pigs can eat high-quality rabbit pellets, but they need additional vitamin C. Supplements of bell peppers, tomatoes, and oranges (high in vitamin C) won't hurt your rabbit either. Their antibiotic sensitivities are similar.

The same veterinarian who sees your rabbit will also be familiar with guinea pigs. If you choose a guinea pig companion for your rabbit, you should familiarize yourself with the special needs of that species as well (see page 94). Have your veterinarian recommend reading material. ∎

Sharing chew toys: *Branches are suitable for both guinea pigs and rabbits.*

PHOTOGRAPHS, ABOVE: AMY ESPIE, OPPOSITE PAGE: HUGH DOUGLAS; INSET: TANIA HARRIMAN

The physical and psychological needs of rabbits are closely related. If you know one, you will soon become acquainted with the other. Knowledge of both will help you to keep your rabbit in good condition for many years.

Dorothy with toy airplane. Joyce Haven (inset) with Celeste at the airport.

FEEDING FOR LONGEVITY

WE USE FOOD TO WIN our rabbits' friendship. We bribe them with edible gifts and encourage them to beg for a treat. We take pleasure in seeing them full-bellied and kicked back on the hearth contentedly. Then we are told that they are overweight.

Domestic rabbits, like their wild cousins, are able to consume large quantities of organic material. Wild rabbits eat succulent grass and clover in the spring—dried grass or straw later in the year. They eat cultivated crops grown for feedstuffs and garden vegetables grown for humans. They eat the fruit that falls from trees, as well as bark from the trees themselves. At times, wild rabbits must survive on twigs and shrubs that are nutritionally low quality to other animals. To do this, they must consume a large volume and convert it to higher quality protein and energy.

Rabbits are voracious eaters. And as much as they love to eat, they also love to forage. This is built in to their survival instinct. Feeding your house rabbit is more than fulfilling nutritional re-

quirements. You are feeding a little psyche. You accomplish this not only by measuring pellets into a bowl but also by stashing high-bulk, low-calorie chewables around the house for bunny to find. That's part of the program.

THE YOUNG DIET

Any diet plan should be appropriate to age and metabolism. Young rabbits can be fed pelleted feed and hay free-choice, or *ad libitum.* (For hand feeding orphan babies see chapter 7.) If you have a "weaned" baby who is less than 7 weeks old, keep the diet very simple. This is a transitional time, in which the sterile intestines are being introduced to bacteria. The baby rabbit must establish healthy intestinal flora in order to survive, and the process should not be rushed.

Rabbit pellets (that don't contain fatty or sugary treats) are the safest choice for youngsters. Purchase them from a reputable pet supply or feed store. If properly stored, the "shelf life" of dry pellets can be as long as 6 months. Rancid or moldy pellets can cause serious illness or death, so store them in a suitable container in a cool dry place after you've opened the package.

TABLE 1: Beginner Diets for Babies and "Teenagers"

Birth to 3 weeks	Mother's milk
3 to 4 weeks	Mother's milk, nibbles of alfalfa hay and pellets
4 to 7 weeks	Mother's milk , free access to alfalfa hay and pellets
7 weeks to 7 mos.	Unlimited pellets, unlimited hay, small amounts of fruit and vegetables introduced one at a time
7 mos. to 1 year	Introduce grass hay and oat hay, decrease alfalfa, start rationing pellets.

PHOTOGRAPH: QUAK WAN-LING

"Bunnies who live in human homes are given many table foods."

THE ADULT DIET

A good time to determine your rabbit's ideal weight for his/her bone structure is at one year old. If you know the right weight for your rabbit, you can then work on maintaining that weight for a lifetime.

TABLE 2: Daily Energy Requirements for Adult Rabbits to Maintain Optimum Body Weight

Body wt lbs	2	3	4	5	6	7	8	9	10
Calories	89	120	149	170	202	227	251	274	296

Based on average of several studies estimating maintenance requirements of New Zealand Whites. (Cheeke 1987, 70–71)

Dietary needs for most species change with maturity. Since mature rabbits tend to put on excess weight, they generally require less of everything—except fiber. Nutritional requirements are more than adequately met with commercial rabbit feeds. Pellets were originally developed for livestock with an emphasis on production, but some manufacturers produce "maintenance" varieties.

Pellet ingredients are listed on the bag. These ingredients are formulated to arrive at the percentages, also listed on the bag, of protein, fiber, and additional vitamins and minerals. They often leave off calories, or digestible energy (DE), which is quite important if you are rationing pellets.

A cup of brand "X" pellets at 950 calories per lb is not equal to a cup of brand "Y" at 1350 calories per lb. Pellet size and density also varies. One brand might be 4 cups per lb, while another might be 3 cups per lb.

TABLE 3. Comparison of Two Pellet Samples

BRAND "X"	BRAND "Y"
950 calories in 1 pound	1350 calories in 1 pound
4 cups = 1 pound (pellet density is coarse)	3 cups = 1 pound (pellet density is fine)
1 cup brand "X"= 238 calories (950/4=238)	1 cup brand "Y"=450 calories (1350/3=450)

PHOTOGRAPH: BOB HARRIMAN

Table approval: *Bunnies like their salads just the way we do—fresh, crisp, and juicy (leave off the dressing).*

Call or write to your pellet manufacturer, to get the number of calories per pound of pellets (kcal/lb). Weigh them yourself to get the number of cups to a pound of *your* pellets. Divide the cups by the calories to get the number of calories in one cup (see Table 3). Then divide energy needs by the calories in a cup to get the amount of that brand to use.

For example, a 7-pound rabbit needs about ½ cup brand "Y" pellets to meet her daily energy requirement of 227 calories.

  1 cup =450 calories (from Table 3)
  Energy needed =227calories (from Table 2)
  (227/450=.50)

These calculations are assuming you are rationing pellets alone, which is seldom the case. Bunnies who live in human homes are given many table foods. Keeping a record of your rabbit's weight is a good way to see that her individual (higher or lower) energy needs are being met. The diet can be adjusted accordingly.

TABLE 4: Energy, protein, fiber, and calcium in several feedstuffs per one-ounce servings

FRESH PRODUCE	DRY MAT. (%)	ENERGY (calories)	PROTEIN (%)	PROTEIN (g)	FIBER (%)	FIBER (g)	CALCIUM (%)	CALCIUM (mg)
Apple	21	20	0.5	.1	1.2	.3	.01	3
Artichoke (Jerus.)	19	17	1.7	.5	.8	.2	.00	—
Banana	24	24	1.1	.3	.5	.1	.01	3
Beets	20	22	1.5	.4	1.5	0.4	.05	14
Cabbage	12	8	2.2	.6	2.0	0.6	.08	23
Carrot tops	17	—	2.7	.8	1.9	0.5	.32	91
Carrots	12	14	1.2	.3	1.1	0.3	.04	11
Celery	6	4	0.9	.3	.6	0.2	.04	11
Dandelion greens	15	8	2.8	.8	1.7	0.5	.20	57
Kale	15	9	3.1	.9	2.0	0.6	.24	68
Lettuce, green	5	3	1.2	.3	.6	0.2	.05	14
Turnip	8	—	1.6	.5	.9	0.3	.04	11
HAYS & GRAINS								
Alfalfa hay	90	51	15.3	4.3	27.0	7.7	1.35	383
Barley grain	89	88	10.7	3.0	5.5	1.6	.06	17
Barley straw*	91	45	4.0	1.1	38.0	10.8	.30	85
Bermuda grass hay	92	47	11.0	3.1	27.6	7.8	.38	108
Clover hay red	88	50	17.3	4.9	21.8	6.2	1.28	364
Clover hay white	92	58	21.4	6.1	20.9	5.9	1.75	497
Corn (heat treated)	88	99	9.2	2.6	2.3	0.7	.04	11
Lespedeza hay	92	37	12.7	3.6	28.1	8.0	.92	261
Oats grain	90	77	11.1	3.2	11.3	3.2	.03	9
Oat hay	88	57	7.3	2.1	29.5	8.4	.25	71
Orchard grass fresh	27	15	3.8	1.1	6.9	2.0	.07	20
Prairie hay*	92	47	5.3	1.5	31.0	8.8	.0	0
Ryegrass hay	89	59	3.8	1.1	33.0	9.4	.45	128
Sudan grass hay*	91	53	7.3	2.1	33.0	9.4	.50	142
Sunflower seeds	92	94	17.1	4.9	22.3	6.3	.20	57
Timothy hay	80	57	6.3	1.8	30.2	8.6	.20	57
Wheat straw*	89	38	3.2	.9	37.0	10.5	.15	43

Table 4 is adapted from Rabbit Feeding and Nutrition (Cheeke 1987) with specifically rabbit values unless otherwise noted.

*United States-Canadian Tables of Feed Composition (not necessarily for rabbits)

NUTRITION WITHOUT EXCESS

As much as your bun needs digestible material, he also needs a large quantity of less digestible fiber. Hay and straw provide both, but select them carefully. Pellets already have large amounts of digestible protein and more than enough calcium and vitamin-D. Alfalfa and clover hays are usually too high in protein and calcium to be given in large amounts to mature non-breeding rabbits in conjunction with pellets.

Prolonged excess calcium and vitamin-D risks damage to rabbits' kidneys. The calcium recommendation for non-breeding rabbits is about .6% of the total diet. (Lebas 1980) Some pellets are formulated to fall within this range, but the total dietary level goes up when alfalfa hay is added.

MIXED DIETS

In putting together a diet of mixed ingredients, a kitchen or postal scale and a calculator or spreadsheet are handy. In determining amounts by weights, you are in for a few surprises. Raw leafy vegetables don't weigh a lot. Throw a handful of dandelion greens onto your kitchen scale and you won't have more than an ounce. Two ounces of hay is a very large handful and as much as a single rabbit will eat in a day. (Three ounces is about a shoebox full!)

Nutritional values in dried hays vary greatly with the season and the cut—making it difficult to meet protein requirements *consistently* on a pelletless diet. (Low listings in Table 4 are likely due to late cuts.) Wild rabbits have access to many forages that meet their protein needs, but these can't be added to your shopping list—like the inner bark of a maple tree. Protein requirement is usually expressed as a percentage of the total diet. However, a more accurate way is in ratio to the calories consumed. (Cheeke 1987, 57)

"Fresh fruits and vegetables are a welcome addition to nearly any diet plan."

Human food values for vegetables are given in cups of chopped or cooked contents—not the way we feed our rabbits. Cup equivalents are listed in the sample menus for fresh foods that we give to rabbits whole—maybe in a less confusing way— by weight. My rabbits consume quantities ranging from 3 to 10 ounces a day, depending on the size of the rabbit and the moisture of the food.

Fresh fruits and vegetables are a welcome addition to nearly any diet plan. Most of what you find in the produce section of the supermarket is OK for your rabbit. Cabbage, cauliflower, rape,

kale, and mustard, although high in goitrogens, are unlikely to cause goiter in rabbits because of the iodized salt in pellets. If you give these veggies without pellets you may need to add some iodized salt from your table.

Never offer a rabbit raw beans, raw corn, potato peels, rhubarb, or any scraps that are too old to eat yourself. Your rabbit is much less able to tolerate spoiled food than you are—and mold is lethal.

If your rabbit has a weight problem, avoid giving any starches or sweets altogether. A more immediate reason for at least limiting starch and

TABLE 5: SAMPLE DAILY MENUS FOR 8 TO 9-LB RABBITS USING PELLETS

MENU 1/ BRAND X PELLETS
GUARANTEED ANALYSIS: Calories = 950 kcal/lb; volume = 4 cups/lb; protein = 16%; fiber = 25%; calcium = .9%

ITEM	WET WT (oz)	DRY WT (oz)	ENERGY (calories)	PROTEIN (g)	PROTEIN (%)	FIBER (g)	FIBER (%)	CALCIUM (mg)	CALCIUM (%)
PELLETS: *1/2 cup*	2.0	1.8	119	9.1	7.9	15.3	12.0	511	.44
OAT HAY : *1 large handful*	2.0	1.8	114	4.1	3.6	16.8	14.3	142	.11
ROLLED OATS: *1/8 cup*	.3	.2	19	.8	.7	.8	.7	2	.00
DANDELION GREENS:*1/2 cup*	1.0	.2	8	.8	.7	.5	.4	57	.05
CARROT:*1small*	1.0	.1	14	.3	.3	.3	.3	11	.01
TOTALS	6.3	4.1	273	15.2	13.1	33.7	27.7	723	.61
APPROXIMATE REQUIREMENTS	—	—		15.0	13.0	18.4+	16.0+	691	.60

MENU 2/ BRAND Y PELLETS
GUARANTEED ANALYSIS: Calories=1350 kcal/lb; volume=3 cups/lb; protein = 18%; fiber = 20%; calcium = .6%

ITEM	WET WT (oz)	DRY WT (oz)	ENERGY (calories)	PROTEIN (g)	PROTEIN (%)	FIBER (g)	FIBER (%)	CALCIUM (mg)	CALCIUM (%)
PELLETS: *1/4 cup*	1.5	1.4	127	7.7	7.6	8.5	8.4	256	.21
TIMOTHY HAY : *1 medium handful*	1.5	1.3	86	2.7	2.7	13.2	13.9	85	.11
ALFALFA HAY : *1 small handful*	.5	.5	26	2.2	2.2	3.9	3.8	192	.19
MIXED GREENS:*1 cup chopped*	2.0	.3	19	1.8	1.7	1.1	1.1	130	.14
BANANA: *1-inch slice*	.5	.1	12	.2	.2	.1	.1	1	.00
TOTALS	6.0	3.6	268	14.4	14.3	26.7	27.3	664	.65
APPROXIMATE REQUIREMENTS	—	—		14.8	14.6	16.2+	16.0+	606	.60

Protein requirements are based on 55 mg per calorie consumed. Percentages, however, are based on dry weight totals.

Safely Reducing Weight in Rabbits

SUSAN SMITH

So you've fed Thumper too many graham crackers and banana chips, and now your vet tells you that she's overweight. What do you do? Just as in humans, it's important to your rabbit's health to maintain an ideal body weight. Obese

rabbits find it difficult to reach their cecal pellets and clean themselves. They also are at risk for diabetes, liver disease, and heart attacks. Restricting pellets and feeding more hay and veggies is a good way to help your rabbit to lose weight and keep it off.

Just like people, rabbits should lose weight slowly and safely. That is, no more than 1-2% of their body weight should be lost per week. This means, for example, that it should take two and one half to five months (from 10 to 20 weeks) for five pound Thumper to lose that extra pound. This slower weight reduction helps your rabbit to readjust her metabolism to this new diet. And, of course, exercise is important too.

Our concern is that some rabbits can develop fatty liver disease (hepatic steatosis) if their weight or food intake declines abruptly. A similar disease is sometimes seen in dieting cats, and it can occur anytime from 24 hours to weeks after a sudden decline in caloric intake. While the acute disease can be detected by monitoring serum liver enzyme levels, some animals can get fatty liver disease and still have normal levels of serum liver enzymes.

What is the solution? Instead of abruptly switching Thumper from unlimited pellets to hay and veggies, gradually reduce her pellet feedings while supplying unlimited hay. Carefully mon-itor your rabbit's weight. Add new veggies to her diet one at a time. By giving Thumper time to adjust to her new diet, both she and you will be rewarded with good health and a more active companion.■

Susan Smith is Assistant Professor, Department of Nutritional Sciences, University of Wisconsin, Madison, with a PhD in biochemistry.

PHOTOGRAPH: MARINELL HARRIMAN

sweet treats is that excesses can cause very serious illness or even death (see chapter 7).

Oats and barley in small amounts are digestible to rabbits, but don't offer corn. (The corn listed in pellet ingredients has been processed to make it digestible.) Refined sugar in candy or cookies is a dangerous treat, and should *not* be given to a rabbit. Surprisingly, however, adult rabbits easily digest fructose, or fruit sugar, (Buddington 1990) so fresh fruit can be given if the calories are under control and the fruit is not overly ripe. Avoid all "bunny treats" that contain sugars and/or fats, such as seeds, nuts, or fried banana.

The guidelines for what to feed and how much, at what ages, are much easier to understand if you know *why*. The very complicated process of rabbit digestion is discussed in more detail in chapter 7.   ∎

TABLE 6: SAMPLE DAILY MENUS FOR 8 TO 9-LB RABBITS USING HAY AND FRESH PRODUCE

MENU 3/ ALFALFA HAY AND OAT HAY BASED

ITEM	WET WT (oz)	DRY WT (oz)	ENERGY (calories)	PROTEIN (g)	PROTEIN (%)	FIBER (g)	FIBER (%)	CALCIUM (mg)	CALCIUM (%)
ALFALFA HAY: *Medium handful*	1.0	.9	51	4.3	4.0	7.7	7.0	383	.35
OAT HAY: *Large handful*	2.0	1.8	114	4.1	3.8	16.8	13.5	142	.11
ROLLED OATS: *1/8 cup*	.3	.2	19	.8	.7	.8	.7	2	.00
ROLLED BARLEY: *1/8 cup*	.3	.2	22	.8	.7	.4	.4	4	.00
DANDELION GREENS: *1 1/2 cups*	3.0	.5	24	2.4	2.2	1.4	1.3	170	.15
CARROT: *1 small*	1.0	.1	14	.3	.3	.3	.3	11	.01
CELERY: *1/2 cup*	1.0	.1	8	.3	.2	.2	.2	11	.01
APPLE: *1-inch wedge*	.5	.1	10	.1	.1	.2	.2	1	.00
TOTALS	9.0	3.8	262	13.1	12.0	27.7	23.5	726	.64
APPROXIMATE REQUIREMENTS	—	—	—	14.4	13.2	17.5+	16.0+	655	.60

MENU 4/ TIMOTHY HAY AND BARLEY STRAW BASED

ITEM	WET WT (oz)	DRY WT (oz)	ENERGY (calories)	PROTEIN (g)	PROTEIN (%)	FIBER (g)	FIBER (%)	CALCIUM (mg)	CALCIUM (%)
TIMOTHY HAY: *1 large handful*	2.0	1.8	114	3.6	3.5	17.2	15.4	114	.00
BARLEY STRAW: *Small handful*	1.0	.9	45	1.1	1.0	10.8	8.7	85	.07
ROLLED BARLEY : *1/2 cup*	.5	.4	44	1.5	1.2	.8	.6	9	.01
BEETS: *1-inch chunk*	1.0	.2	14	.4	.4	.4	.3	14	.01
CARROT: *1 medium*	2.0	.2	2	.7	.0	.6	.5	23	.02
MIXED GREENS: *2 cups*	4.0	.6	35	3.5	2.9	2.3	1.9	227	.22
APPLE: *1-inch wedge*	.5	.1	10	.1	.1	.2	.1	1	.00
TOTALS	11.0	4.3	264	10.9	9.1	32.2	27.7	473	.34
APPROXIMATE REQUIREMENTS	—	—	—	14.5	11.9	19.4+	16.0+	729	.60

Protein requirements are based on 55 mg per calorie consumed. Percentages, however, are based on dry weight totals.

EXERCISING

IN RECENT YEARS, we have become more convinced than ever of the importance of exercise in maximizing the life expectancy of domestic rabbits. Exercise is good for physical and mental health. Like other household animals, rabbits can easily become sedentary. You can spend time playing games with them, but they also need encouragement to exercise on their own. How can ex-ercise be encouraged? By providing uncaged time/space and catalysts for activity.

Climbing up or jumping out:
Seagull (inset) gets some exercise on a stack of wicker baskets while Agarami takes advantage of a door intentionally left open.

EXERCISE SPACE

Adequate space for exercise can be provided in a number of places—a single room, an entire house, a porch or balcony, or a secure outdoor playpen. It's not so much a matter of huge amounts of space but rather what is put into that space to stimulate the bunnies into action.

You might find that a smaller space with lots of things to do better serves the purpose than turn-

PHOTOGRAPHS, INSET: CAROLYN LONG, RIGHT: RACHAEL MILLAN VASTINE

Bridges to playgrounds: *Leonard descends a louvered ramp (short toenails only) to his daytime run; Abby (inset) climbs her rug-covered ramp to an indoor play area.*

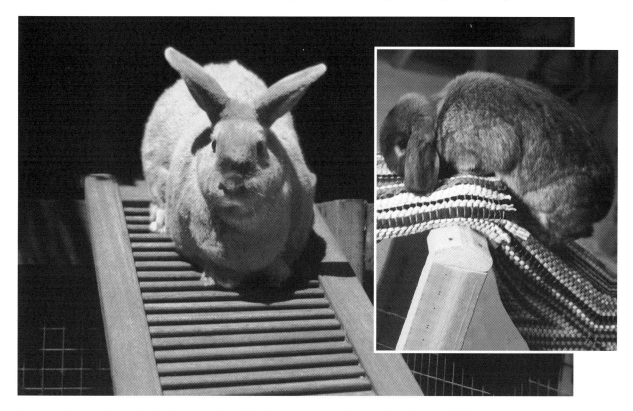

ing your bunny loose in the backyard and risking many dangers. Once you have decided on a safe area to exercise your bunny, you only need to add engaging, full-body exercise equipment. It may be nothing more than things bunnies like to climb onto or jump off of.

Boxes and baskets may be considered chew toys, but in a stack, they can stimulate some climbing or digging action. Rabbits enjoy running up and down ramps and through tunnels. We highly recommend both of these for rabbit gymnasiums. Our foster rabbits use ramps to get from the house to their daytime playpens. Ramps can also be used in cages and indoor running spaces. Set them up in any area where bunny must climb to get to a favorite place.

Cardboard tubes (concrete forms), found in building supply stores, make great rabbit tunnels. Or you can purchase a carpeted cat tunnel from your pet supply store. Use your imagination to create your bunny's gymnasium and have some fun yourself. ∎

PHOTOGRAPHS, LEFT: BOB HARRIMAN, INSET: CAROLYN LONG

OUTDOOR SAFETY

A COMPLETELY SAFE OUTDOOR HUTCH seldom exists. Even when elevated several feet off the ground, wire cages do not prevent the possibility of self-induced trauma or shock due to fright from imminent predators.

Running loose in the yard, a rabbit is all the more likely to come in contact with predators. Also there is danger from toxic plants,* pesticides, parasites, soil contamination, or moving vehicles.

Predatory animals include stray dogs, feral cats, large birds, foxes, wolves, large reptiles, and raccoons (the most commonly underestimated threats to rabbits). Raccoons come up through storm drains into very urban areas and find prey at night.

A little known fact is that a predator can kill a rabbit without physical contact. All it may take is the presence of the predator—within distance to be seen, smelled, or heard. Whether thrashing in a hutch or fleeing across the yard in panic, the rabbit may incur permanent injury or enter a state of shock that results in death.

DAYTIME SOLUTIONS

A safe outdoor running space for daytime use is a well furnished covered playpen. My husband has built several playpens of 1-inch welded wire, stretched over wooden frames (3 x 8 ft). The wire covers all four sides and the bottom. A thick layer of clean yellow straw covers the wire floor. The rabbits can dig, burrow, push, and shove the straw without major health risks.

The 8-foot length gives the rabbits enough room to kick up their heels and run around. Yet the whole frame is not too heavy for me to turn over for cleaning or to move about in the yard. Plywood tops are attached as protection from daytime predators and direct sunlight.

An enclosed porch or balcony can serve the same purpose. Here, too, there should be full fencing from top to bottom even at upper-story levels, unless you are on hand to supervise. Predatory birds can and do snatch rabbits from balconies, as well as yards.

Whatever arrangement you make for a safe outdoor daytime playground for your bunny, ALWAYS bring him in at night. ∎

A safe place to play: Some California bunnies take themselves down a ramp to their secure enclosure (left). Colorado bunnies are hand carried to a safe play yard by Nancy La Roche and Earl McCullough (right).

Note: Degrees and kinds of toxicity in plants are variable for different species. To find out what plants in your area might be toxic to rabbits, you can contact the National Animal Poison Control Center. See page 94.

PHOTOGRAPHS: TANIA HARRIMAN

GROOMING

PHYSICAL MAINTENANCE OF YOUR RABBIT includes brushing, combing, manicuring, and cleaning. With regular grooming you can prevent several major health problems and save your bunny a trip to the veterinarian.

CARE OF THE COAT

Brushing or combing your rabbit keeps the coat clean and free of burrs, mats and stickers. Brushing your rabbit will also remove loose hair that could otherwise build up in your vacuum cleaner or, worse yet, in your rabbit's stomach (see hairballs in chapter 7). All rabbits shed to some extent, and most will go through a major shed a couple of times a year.

A slicker brush is the one most commonly used for rabbits, although a rubber brush is useful during a shedding period to remove a lot of loose hair. I have come to use a flea comb for the major part of my rabbits' grooming, mainly because they love it! However, if you're working with an extremely matted coat, you will have to use brushes and mat splitters first. Long-haired rabbits require daily brushing. Otherwise their coats can become so hopelessly entangled that you will give up in despair and pay the price of having a groomer do the job for you.

Use a mat rake or mat splitter instead of scissors. Rabbits have delicate skin, which can be easily nicked and cut. If you must use scissors, get a blunt-nosed pair, and don't pull on the fur while you are trimming, or you may cut the skin. Keep the skin very flat, and trim very patiently.

FLEAS/FUR MITES

Even the best groomed bunny who goes outside may pick up fleas or mites. Numerous flea and mite products are available, which can be powdered, sprayed, bombed, or even taken orally. Generally, products safe for kittens are safe for rabbits, but check with your vet for precautions and specific products.

When using powders, start at the neck and work downward, separating about a one-inch section at a time and working it in all the way to the skin, so it doesn't stir up a lot of powder into the air. I powder all areas except the face, where I use a flea comb. During warm weather (flea season), flea powdering can be done once or twice a week.

Flea dips and baths are not recommended for rabbits. This may seem confusing, considering that some rabbits play in wading pools during the summer. What may be a harmless *routine* for some rabbits can be devastating to others. Elderly rabbits

Bunny in a towel: *Susan Stark who has fostered 60-70 rabbits at a time demonstrates an easy grooming position with bunny's head on the knees of the groomer.*

"When bunny's toenails grow too long, they can catch in the carpeting or cage wire."

who are not used to full-body dips or compromised animals with an undetected illness may go into shock when bathed.

SPOT CLEANINGS

Certain areas on a rabbit can be cleaned with appropriate cleansers. An otic *chlorhexidine* solution that dissolves waxy buildup can be used in the ears and swabbed out with cotton. Be careful not to push wax further into the ear canal.

To tend to a rabbit's underside, I use the reverse position to the one on the previous page—with bunny's head against my ribcage. (Try both directions to see what works best with your rabbit.) An over-the-counter chlorhexidine solution can be applied to dirty hindquarters.

If you really must shampoo the area, have running tap water already adjusted to lukewarm temperature, then thrust bunny's rear end under the faucet. Try to keep the feet dry and only soak a minimal area.

My least preferred way, which I resort to only rarely—in such cases as diarrhea, in which the legs and feet have become soiled—is a half bath. This is allowing the lower quarters from the waist down to be completely submerged in warm water. Normal shampooing and rinsing are followed by a thorough towel drying and combing. Sometimes follow-up work with a hair dryer is necessary. If a dirty bottom has become a chronic problem, shaving the area may be the only way to keep it clean and dry.

Keeping bunny dry all over is very important, but especially so around the tail and feet. A wet tail attracts flies which can be a serious health hazard in itself. Excess moisture on the feet can damage exposed skin, leaving it susceptible to infection. This is another reason artificial padding in the form of rugs—*provided they remain dry*—can be beneficial in rabbit housing.

TOENAIL CLIPPING

When bunny's toenails grow too long, they can catch in the carpeting or cage wire. Broken bleeding toenails are very prone to infection that can even invade bony tissue and cause serious damage. Always keep the toenails clipped short. When clipping, avoid cutting into the vein. If you can't see the quick in a dark toenail hold a flashlight behind it. Have a styptic powder on hand (from the pet supply shop) to stop bleeding, just in case.

We absolutely do NOT recommend declawing rabbits. There is serious risk of infection. Don't even consider this as an option. If your rabbit is digging up your carpet (after she has been spayed), give her a large hay box and let her dig to her heart's content. ∎

Hard as nails? *You can locate the quick (inset) before cutting. For dark nails, you can backlight them with a flashlight.*

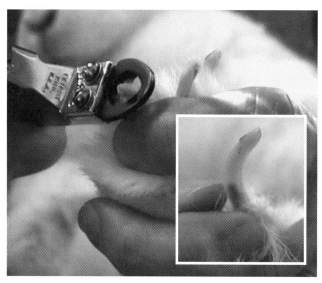

VIDEOGRAPH: MARINELL HARRIMAN

"These short periods keep the experience pleasant for both of you."

The Well Kept Rabbit

SANDI ACKERMAN

THE KEY TO GIVING your rabbit the best chance for a long life, is to provide a happy environment and to spot problems early. Here are some life-extending procedures:

DAILY ROUTINES

Hug your rabbit and as you do, become familiar with his body. You don't have to pick him up to do this, you can hug him while he and you are on the floor together. As you hug, feel him all over. Caress along his jaw line—then feel his tummy. Caress his head—then feel the crook of his legs and arms. Play "smushy face" with his entire head—then feel under his chin. You get the idea—something that feels good, then something that may feel strange to him, at least the first few times you do this. He'll soon just think this is part of human behavior and will at first just put up with it and then learn to like it. What you are doing is getting used to the normal feel of his body, where his usual lumps and bumps are and what they feel like. Then, if anything changes you'll be aware of it.

Keeping in touch: Anita Richter of Chicago stays lovingly acquainted with Nadia's intricacies.

Check his litterbox, looking for changes in the size or shape of his hard round droppings which can indicate an intestinal problem. Seeing some hair strung between droppings is normal when he's shedding, but if you see very thick hair between the droppings then you should read about hairballs again, just to make sure you're doing all that you can to help him pass the hair out of his stomach. And of course, make sure that he's been urinating. If you find very thick white or grey urine for more than a day or two, he may have too much calcium in his diet.

Bonding and grooming go together. In order to keep hair from flying around your home and from being ingested by your rabbit, for just a couple of minutes every day, comb or brush your rabbit. These short periods keep the experience pleasant for both of you. Within a short time he will likely begin to look forward to these few minutes of daily bonding.

Other daily tasks include supplying fresh water and pellets, fresh veggies and small amounts of fruit, and plenty of hay.

WEEKLY TASKS

Clean his living area thoroughly.
Check eyes & nose to see that there is no discharge.
Check inside ears to see if they look clean far down inside.

EVERY OTHER MONTH

Clip nails.
Check bottom of feet for sores.
Check teeth to see that they're properly aligned.
Clean genital scent glands (one on either side of the genitals).
Check scent gland under the chin. As rabbits age this area can become infected.
Check for fleas.
Check for dandruff (could be mites).

Keeping up with these health promoting tasks will mean a well kept rabbit. None of these things will take a lot of your time, but his time with you and the quality of both of your lives, can be greatly increased. ∎

PHOTOGRAPH: ROBERT RICHTER

WELL KEPT ENVIRONMENT

Hairy office in Oregon: *Darla shares space in Kathy Kifer's home-office/ studio. This kind of arrangement requires more vacuuming, but people do it anyway.*

WHENEVER WE ARE ASKED to talk about rabbit husbandry, our reply is, "We don't do husbandry. These are companions, not farm animals." On the other hand, we have a lot to say about maintaining adequate living arrangements. Recommendations for sterilizing cages only apply to rabbitries or institutions that keep a large number of rabbits in cages. Any animal who sits day after day in a cage will require a different kind of hygiene than free-running house rabbits.

Our house rabbits, who run about on our carpets, beg at our tables, and hop into our beds, require the same amount of cleanliness for good health as our other companion animals. Care should be taken, however, to keep any spoiled or rancid food off the floor (e.g. knocked-over waste baskets). Things that may be perfectly harmless to your dog can be deadly to your rabbit.

Regular vacuuming and mopping are necessary with any furry animal. Many rabbits spend time in (bunny-proof) computer rooms. Frequent vacuuming around and even inside your computer is advisable. It's amazing how much fly-around hair from cats and rabbits can get inside your computer.

An occasional scattered "marble" can be swept up with a whisk broom, between vacuumings. For urine accidents on carpeting, upholstery, or bedspreads, use white vinegar, the all-purpose cleaner for rabbit environments. The acidity of vinegar discourages bacteria growth and does a good job of neutralizing the highly alkaline rabbit urine. Use wood soap on hardwood floors where vinegar can't be used.

USEFUL CLEANUP TOOLS/SUPPLIES

vacuum cleaner	litter spatula (metal)
small hand vacuum	paint scraper/spatula
whisk broom & dustpan	scrub brush
mop	white vinegar
sponge	paper towels
bottle brush	wood soap

Maintenance of bunny's personal possessions starts with the cage. Line the tray with newspaper or litter. The top and sides will need occasional vacuuming to remove clinging hair. The cage floor may sometimes require a vinegar scrub.

The only time you need to disinfect with chlorine bleach is after an illness, after surgery, or before the cage is occupied by a new rabbit.

"...let your neighbor with the rose garden know about your supply of rabbit fertilizer."

WATER AND PELLET UTENSILS

Fresh water must be available at all times. Bowls or crocks should be rinsed daily and re-filled. Rinse and refill bottles after two days, but check them daily for leakage or plugging. Lids on older bottles can be unclogged with a wire coat hanger. Or better yet replace older bottles. Scrub all water bottles or crocks with a brush and hot soapy water once a month.

Dump pellet bowls daily. Hanging feeders with screen bottoms allow small particles of feed to sift through. Feeders with solid bottoms have to be removed and dumped the same as a bowl.

Besides being convenient, large plastic storage containers, with tight fitting lids, preserve the freshness of pellets and hay and keep out bugs and other pests. Keep the boxes in a cool area.

THE LITTERBOX

Use rabbit-safe organic litter (discussed in chapter 2). Handy litter scoops can be cut from empty vinegar jugs. One scoop of litter is about the right amount for a small litterbox. One scoop will last a single rabbit two days' use. The box can be topped with another scoop and last another two days. The litterbox will need to be changed after four days' use. A box shared by two rabbits will need to be changed after two days' use. To prevent mineral build-up rinse the box with vinegar every time it is changed.

A small litterbox is easy to tip over and might need to be attached to the cage. To attach it, punch or drill a hole in the side. Insert a wire tie (like the ones that come with your plastic trash bags), then twist-tie it to the side of the cage.

HAY/STRAW AS LITTER

If you don't want bunny's hay used as litter material, keep it in a hay rack. If you do want it used for litter you need size—a large hay tub and a large amount of grass-hay or straw. A well layered hay box, with newspaper on the bottom and a clean hay/straw topping daily, will last a week.

LITTER DISPOSAL

Organic litters make disposal quite easy. Most can be dumped right into your garden or added to your compost pile and, combined with rabbit manure, make excellent fertilizer.

If you have no yard, the lightweight pulp litters do not overload your household garbage can. Or let your neighbor with the rose garden know about your supply of rabbit fertilizer. ∎

Multi-purpose: *Furry dusty areas need frequent vacuuming (left) Wire ties prevent litter tip-over (middle). Clean with vinegar and cut a scoop from the empty jug (right).*

OCCASIONAL NEEDS

SOME RABBITS LIKE to travel, others do not. If you do a lot of recreational traveling, it would be advisable to get bunny used to traveling with you. Many precautions must be practiced, however. Don't travel without air-conditioning during hot weather, and never leave your rabbit in an unshaded parked car. Avoid driving in congested traffic during "rush hours." Rabbits have been known to succumb to exhaust fumes from prolonged exposure while riding on the floor next to the "fresh-air" vents (quite a misnomer when driving in air-polluted areas).

Depending on your destination, you might want to consider taking a portable playpen or a harness and leash to use once you have arrived. Bunny can be fitted for a harness at your pet supply store prior to your trip.

When bunny is walking you, keep the leash fairly short and held high to prevent tangling around small shrubs. Rabbits panic when trapped in a tangled leash. A rabbit should never be left on a leash unattended. Avoid having bunny play in well-cultivated public parks that have been re-

cently sprayed with pesticides or weed killers.

Most people don't take their rabbits on unnecessary trips on commercial airlines. If you are moving across country, however, it may be necessary. The rules seem to change from day to day, but some airlines allow you to have bunny's carrier in the cabin with you. If you must use cargo, check on temperature control. You might also want to send for the article, "To Fly or Not to Fly," from HRS (address on page 94).

NON TRAVELING OPTIONS

When you must be away from home for several days or more, your first choice is to have family members or friends look after your bunny in your absence. The next best thing to having a bunny-sitter who knows *your* rabbit is to have one who knows rabbits in general.

A veterinary bulletin board is one place to look for a pet-sitter. Check on what suits your needs best. Some do actual house-sitting. Others will come in at specified times to feed and exercise your animals. Others may board your animal on their own premises. If you choose boarding, you will want to see the facilities. Check for kennel cleanliness and exercise accommodations.

Competent pet-sitters are familiar with health needs of the species that they're working with. Most are experienced at giving injections and can follow any program that your veterinarian has prescribed.

One thing I recommend is to leave a check made out to your veterinary hospital in case of an emergency while you are away. I learned this from my daughter, Tania, who does rabbit-sitting. Instead of frightening people away, this policy has caused people to relax, knowing that their rabbit's condition will be closely watched and that any necessary veterinary care will be obtained. ∎

PHOTOGRAPHS, ABOVE: AMY ESPIE, OPPOSITE PAGE: BOB HARRIMAN

Keeping your bunny *alive and well means a watchful program of prevention as well as appropriate attention to illnesses and injuries.*

Your partner in this program is your veterinarian.

Carolynn Harvey, DVM and Wilma make preparations.

BUNNY EXAM

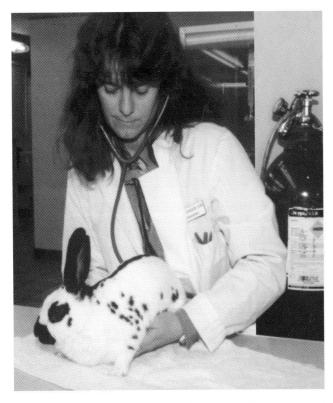

check for respiratory disease, listen to heart and digestive sounds, and palpate the abdomen to check for organ or intestinal abnormalities.

Cancer is very common in unspayed females, especially after their fifth year. It's best to have spay or neuter surgery done well before then.

Listening and feeling for abnormalities:
Dr. Bronwyn Dawson examines the underside of Christopher for symptoms of illness.

Of course, you want the sex determined—something not so easy to do if this is your first rabbit, because the genitals of immature males and females look similar. Unless you adopt an already neutered/spayed rabbit, one of the first exams should be a "pre-operative." Depending on your rabbit's age and health conditions, your veterinarian may recommend a blood panel to check for anemia, kidney function, and liver enzymes. This will help indicate any special precautions that need to be taken. ∎

 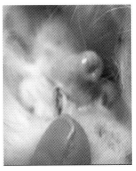

Female: *The vulva can be seen when pressure is applied above the genital area. The protrusion is pointed.*

Male: *The penis is also seen by applying pressure above genitals. The protrusion is round and flat at the end.*

THE NEXT PRIORITY to knowing what is normal for your rabbit is knowing when to get the professional help of a good rabbit doctor. One of the most important alliances you will ever form to ensure your rabbit's longevity is with your veterinarian. You must be able to work together on bunny's health care program.

Make the first appointment early. Start your bunny with a head-to-toe exam in your veterinarian's office and get a file set up. Then you will be ready if an emergency arises. Your veterinarian will

PHOTOGRAPHS, UPPER LEFT: TIM LABONGE, LOWER RIGHT: MARINELL HARRIMAN

ELECTIVE SURGERY

WHEN SURGERY IS REQUIRED to remove an infection, a tumor, a hairball or a bladder stone, you have no choice but to proceed in order to improve your bunny's chance for survival. On the other hand, spaying or neutering is considered elective surgery, intended to improve behavior and ensure good toilet habits in addition to preventing pregnancies. There are also health benefits, such as fewer bite wounds and scratches from each other and elimination of hormonally-induced infections. And a complete spay, of course, eliminates the risk of uterine cancer. Risk is as high as 80% in 5-year-olds.

IMPROVED TECHNIQUES

Rabbit surgery has become much safer in recent years as veterinarians perform them routinely. Males can be neutered as soon as the testicles have descended. This can happen any time after 3½ months. Females are usually spayed at 4–6 months old, depending on size.

In recent years, the House Rabbit Society has had well over 2,000 rabbits spayed or neutered. Of course we go to experienced veterinarians. We *never* fast our rabbits before or after surgery (they don't vomit). We have seen that rabbits have much better morale, undergo surgery with greater ease, and make a much quicker recovery if they don't miss a meal. Some arguments have been presented in the past that undigested food in the digestive tract will affect the rabbit's weight and therefore the anesthesia dosage. The fact is that you would have to fast a rabbit ten days (not that you would ever want to) in order to completely clear her digestive tract.

Fasting, on the other hand, may cause an interruption in digestive functions, and it sometimes makes it more difficult to get rabbits eating again after the surgery.

PHOTOGRAPH: MARINELL HARRIMAN

SAFELY HANDLED ANESTHESIA

Most veterinary hospitals are now equipped with isoflurane, which is the anesthesia of choice for rabbits. Safety of the procedure, however, does not rest entirely with the anesthesia but with the skill of the practitioner. The isoflurane deaths that were reported to us a few years ago were mostly due to lack of pre-anesthetics and adequate preparations. Veterinarians now have experience using isoflurane, and preparations should no longer be a problem.

Other types of anesthesia can also be used safely on rabbits. Our veterinarians routinely use halothane and so do low-cost neuter clinics. High volume clinics usually acquire such enormous experience that they can use halothane safely. Pre-anesthetics are particularly important, since a combination of adrenaline and halothane can be lethal. If you have an exceptionally nervous high-strung rabbit, be sure to let the surgeon know so that your bunny can be well sedated with pre-anesthetic before

Ear catheter: *Intravenous medications can be given throughout the surgery procedure, if necessary, by having an ear catheter already in place.*

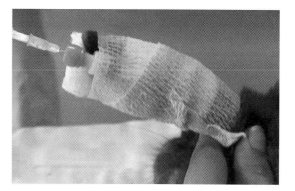

"Veterinarians who do have extensive experience are willing to share their expertise."

the gas is given.

In pointing out possible risk, I have to add that I personally have had hundreds of rabbits spayed or neutered using halothane and have never encountered an anesthetic-related death. While surgery may be safer if done before the rabbit is a year old, we don't always have that age choice. Many of our rescued rabbits were 5-6 years old at the time of surgery. Our veterinarian opted for isoflurane for 10-year-old Sieglinda last year, when uterine cancer mandated surgery. Sieglinda had not been spayed earlier because of compromised health (she survived just fine).

The most important thing is that your veterinarian work with the anesthesia with which he/she is most comfortable and most experienced. A word of encouragement to practitioners who lack experience in rabbit surgery. Veterinarians who do have extensive experience are willing to share their expertise. Most of them can be contacted for advice

POST-OPERATIVE CARE

This is one of the few times that a cage needs to be disinfected. Your bunny should be confined to a cage for a few days to prevent overdoing: 2 days for males; about 5 or 6 days for females. Provide comfortable bedding , such as a synthetic sheepskin rug, so that there will be no inclination to sleep in the litterbox (and contaminate the suture area). Mixed sexes should be separated for about 2 weeks, in case of stored sperm (unless the female is already spayed), and also to allow incisions to heal before engaging in any sexual activity. Yes, many neutered pairs continue to be sexually active.

Usually, no antibiotic is necessary if the suture area is kept clean and there are no signs of infection. Check the sutures daily.

Most bunnies are able to eat immediately, but some may be anorexic for a couple of days. (This is more likely if the bunny has fasted prior to surgery.) Hay is especially good to feed at this time to get the digestive system moving again.   ∎

Suture removal: *All's well for big Belle, ten days after she was rushed to the hospital for emergency spay (due to profuse bleeding).*

PHOTOGRAPH: BOB HARRIMAN

MIN-MIN GETS SPAYED

THE WORLD HAS BECOME SMALLER since the birth of the Internet. Rabbit people no longer feel isolated for not living next door to another person with similar enthusiasm for rabbits. They are meeting each other all over the world.

Sandi Ackerman of the Seattle branch of the House Rabbit Society met Wan-Ling on the Internet a year and a half ago, when Wan-Ling's rabbit, Min-Min, had cancer. Her veterinarian in Singapore had been treating Min-Min for a bladder infection for the previous 6 months, because of blood in the urine (which always appeared at the end of urinating). When Sandi heard about it, she thought it was likely to be cancer and suggested that 6-year-old Min-Min should be spayed.

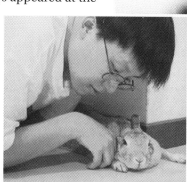

Since Min-Min's veterinarian had never done a spay on a rabbit before, she called Dr. Susan Brown of Chicago and received instructions from her over the phone and via fax. The surgery was done, and Min-Min survived. She definitely did prove to have cancer, but fortunately it had not spread. Beautiful healthy Min-Min has resumed her pampered lifestyle.

Wan-Ling brought Min-Min with her when she returned from school in Tokyo to live with her mother and sister in Singapore 6 ½ years ago. Her mother was not thrilled at the idea of living with a house rabbit, but things did change with time.

Wan-Ling and her sister, Heoi-Ling, (page 16) enjoy romping with Min-Min every evening after work. (Wan-Ling is a software engineer for Sony, and Heoi-Ling is a merchandiser for Gap.) Their mother is self-assigned as Min-Min's cage cleaner.

They are happy to have found a veterinarian interested in rabbits in their part of the world and a world-wide community of rabbit people. ■

Petting time. *A fully recovered Min-Min gets attention from her human, Wan-Ling, (above) and awaits new adventures (right).*

PHOTOGRAPHS: QUAK WAN-LING

DIGESTIVE PROCESSING

THE RABBIT DIGESTIVE SYSTEM is truly amazing. If you make an effort to understand how it works, you will be able to prevent many illnesses that result from improper feeding.

INTESTINAL FORTITUDE

The standard churning and mixing process in the stomach is similar to that of other animals, but the intestines handle the food much differently.

The small intestine. The very long length of the rabbit small intestine is where most nutrients are absorbed. Sugars and starches are absorbed here and also up to 90% of the ingested protein. Rabbits do not digest cellulose, or plant cells, efficiently in the small intestine, (Gidenne 1992) but they have an alternate way of dealing with this major part of their diet. Material passes from the small intestine to the cecum and colon. Then it is processed according to size.

The cecum. Contractions of the fermenting vat, or cecum, keep large particles pushed out. Small particles of cellulose are retained for fermentation, along with excess sugar, starch and protein from the small intestine. Fermentation means di-

gesting by bacteria. The cecum is filled with beneficial, food-digesting bacteria and protozoa.

The colon. The large intestine, or colon, does some unique things in rabbits. In addition to forming fecal pellets, it separates small particles in the *haustral* section and sends them backwards into the cecum. (Haustrae are sacculations formed by circular muscles.)

Large-fiber particles are sent on their way for quick passage through the colon to become the large hard marbles that you see in your bunny's litterbox. Contrary to what you might expect, the large-fiber particles don't get stuck inside the rabbit while the small ones exit easily. It's the other way around.

RECYCLING PLAN

The fermentation process in the cecum produces volatile fatty acids, which are absorbed directly into the bloodstream. The cecum also produces B-complex vitamins and protein to be reingested. The vitamin/protein-rich material from the cecum is packaged into little clusters of *cecotropes* while passing through the colon.

Cecotropes are an important part of your bunny's diet. They are enclosed in a protective membrane, allowing them to ferment several more hours in the stomach after they are reingested. Finally the nutrients in the cecotropes are ready to be absorbed.

That's a pretty elaborate, round-about way of getting nourishment out of a blade of grass or the apple tree branch your bunny has been nibbling on (or your baseboard), but it works for wild rabbits who must get the most out of the poor food sources that are available. This is the way that nature has designed for them. In this complicated plan of processing and reprocessing, a rabbit's digestive tract must be constantly moving.

PHOTOGRAPH: MARINELL HARRIMAN

"…an elaborate, round-about way of getting nourishment…"

FIGURE 1: Rabbit Gastrointestinal Tract

1. Esophagus. Plant food, ground in a sideways motion of the lower jaw, is swallowed and passed to the *stomach* through the esophagus.

2. Stomach. Muscular contractions squeeze and churn the food in a circular path, mixing them with the *gastric fluid* of the stomach, which is kept sterile by certain fatty acids.

3. Duodenum (first part of the *small intestine*). As the food particles exit the stomach, enzymes from the *liver* are secreted into the small intestine at the duodenum.

4. Small Intestine (comprised of the *duodenum, jejunum,* and *ileum*). The major part of digestion takes place during the passage through the small intestine. Some sugars, most starches, and up to 90% of all protein are absorbed, while *cellulose* is not efficiently digested.

5. Ileocecocolonic junction (major crossroads in the intestinal tract). Material passes from the small intestine to the *cecum* and *proximal colon*. Material also passes back and forth between the cecum and proximal colon in continual flux. (Cheeke 1987)

6. Cecum (fermenting vat). Contractions keep large particles moving into the colon. Small particles are retained for fermentation. Bacteria digest

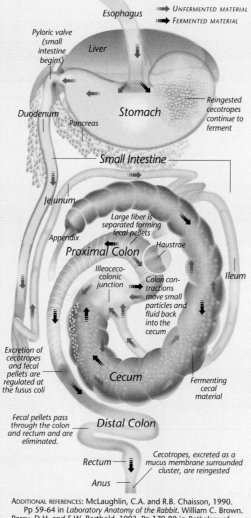

small-fiber cellulose, along with protein, sugars and starches that haven't been digested in the small intestine. B-complex vitamins are produced along with volatile fatty acids, which are absorbed directly into the bloodstream. *Normal flora of the cecum: protozoa* and *anaerobic* bacteria—*Bacteroides sp, streptococcus fecalis,* and *Clostridia sp* (some strains are harmful).

7. Colon. Contractions of the *haustrae* in the proximal colon separate small particles, sending them backward into the cecum. Larger particles are eliminated as hard droppings, or *fecal pellets*. Vitamin-rich cecal material is formed into soft droppings or *cecotropes* .

8. Fusus coli between the proximal and *distal* colon regulates the excretion of hard and soft droppings.

9. Anus. Cecotropes, packaged in mucus-membrane clusters, are consumed directly and returned to the digestive system.

10. Reingested cecotropes. Protected in mucus-membrane packages, cecotropes continue to ferment in the stomach for several hours, until they pass to the small intestine where the nutrients are absorbed. (Cheeke 1987)

CONSULTANTS:

CAROLYNN HARVEY, DVM, KARL WAIDHOFER, DVM, RICHARD EVANS, DVM, MS

ADDITIONAL REFERENCES: McLaughlin, C.A. and R.B. Chaisson, 1990. Pp 59-64 in *Laboratory Anatomy of the Rabbit.* William C. Brown. Percy, D.H. and S.W. Barthold. 1993. Pp 179-80 in *Pathology of Laboratory Rodents and Rabbits.* Iowa State University Press.

"Prevention of both hairballs and impactions is largely dietary."

THE RIGHT MICROBES

A rabbit relies on anaerobic bacteria (grows without oxygen) in the cecum to break down cellulose. If the microbial balance of the cecum is altered by filling up the cecum with sugar or starch, this can cause an overgrowth of harmful bacteria that can make your bunny sick. And not only that—if these harmful bacteria continue to grow, they can produce deadly toxins that will kill your rabbit (enterotoxemia). That's why it is stated in chapter 6 that most starches and all sweet treats should not be in your rabbit's diet. The only exception is fructose, the natural sugar in fruit.

GASTRIC BLOCKAGES

A healthy gastrointestinal (GI) tract is an active one, and illness occurs if any part of it shuts down. Sometimes the upper or gastric area is affected.

Hairballs. Without plenty of fiber, swallowed hair or synthetic material from your home furnishings can block your rabbit's digestive flow. Rabbits don't rid themselves of swallowed hair by vomiting like a cat. It must pass through them. Hair and synthetics that don't pass may form a hairball, or trichobezoar, in the stomach.

Twenty years ago, scientific data seemed to indicate that trichobezoars were common. One study reported, "over a 3-mo. period, 34 of 80 (43%) New Zealand white rabbits died spontaneously with gastric trichobezoars..." (Wagner 1974)

Having read these frightening numbers in the late 1980s, we watched for such problems and then noticed that hairballs were not occurring among our house rabbits. The major causes of gastric hairball—lack of roughage or abnormal fur chewing (due to stress, boredom, inadequate rations)—are not normally present in our house rabbits' lives.

Stomach impaction. A much more common problem in rabbit digestion results from overeating. The stomach can fill with too much low-fiber food, which, combined with even small amounts of hair, can cause an impaction (Brown 1995) that slows or stops motility and mimics a true hairball.

Treatment/prevention. Prevention of both hairballs and impactions is largely dietary. Among long-term preventives are brushing to remove loose hair, plenty of hay, and exercise. A major reason to give your rabbit lots of hay is that large-fiber particles in hay pass quickly through the digestive tract, pushing the hair and other indigestibles right along with them.

Treatment for trichobezoars has traditionally been mineral oil, petroleum cat laxatives, pineapple/papaya enzymes, or surgery. Smaller hairballs may respond to laxative or enzyme treatment. Enzymes do not dissolve hair but may help to dissolve food and mucus that binds the hair together. Sometimes a stomach gavage is used to try to break up the fur mass. This must be done with considerable skill by an adept practitioner so that the tube enters the stomach and not the larynx. Surgery is the last resort. Veterinarians will not attempt this high-risk procedure unless the case is severe and not responding to conservative care.

If your hair-blocked or im-

FIGURE 2: Trichobezoar (hairball)

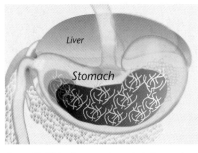

Liver

Stomach

A partial blockage reduces but does not stop digestive flow. This condition can usually be treated without surgery. Complete blockage, however, prevents food intake and usually requires surgical removal.

"Coarse low-digestible organic material keeps the gut working at an optimum rate."

pacted rabbit has stopped eating and drinking, he may need to be hospitalized to receive around-the-clock care, or he may be sent home for you to carry on any or all of the following treatments:

Fluids. These are often given subcutaneously (under the skin), usually twice a day.

Pain medication. If necessary, this will be prescribed for gas discomfort.

Pineapple juice. Fresh or frozen: 9-10 cc by mouth three times a day. The fluid is helpful. The enzymes (bromelain) won't hurt and may help.

Hay. Give any kind the rabbit will eat—to get things moving again.

Fresh produce. Feed leafy greens. These provide much needed moisture along with some fiber. A technique of persuasion is fresh offerings. Have several kinds—broccoli, parsley, carrot tops, dandelion greens, and especially radish tops (the first thing that many anorexic rabbits eat willingly).

Cat laxative. (if your veterinarian decides it is necessary) 3 cc twice a day. This should be done at least a half hour after pineapple juice is given. The intention is to soften the mass before the laxative starts working.

INTESTINAL DISRUPTIONS

Digestive processing can stop also in the lower, GI tract due to impacted cecum and enteritis. The cecum can become impacted for various reasons

Dehydration. This may be due to hot weather, insufficient water intake, ingestion of water absorbing fiber (such as psyllium used in human laxatives) or any absorbent litterbox material. When fluids are needed elsewhere, they are drawn from the cecum's reservoir into the blood, leaving a hard accumulating mass in the cecum.

Overload. If too much low-fiber food is consumed, most of it will pass to the cecum. The cecum spends one to four days (sometimes longer) fer-

menting the material. A portion of the cecal contents is emptied daily, but not all. If more small material enters the cecum than exits, the result may be a cecal impaction. Or the slowdown may alter gut flora enough to cause enteritis.

Coarse low-digestible organic material keeps the gut working at an optimum rate. Scientific studies show that large particles can pass through

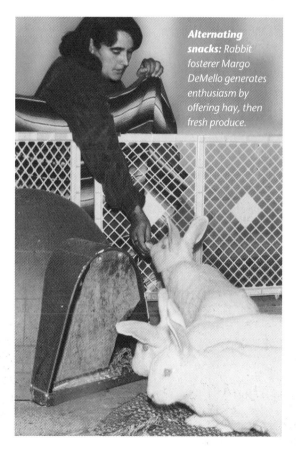

Alternating snacks: Rabbit fosterer Margo DeMello generates enthusiasm by offering hay, then fresh produce.

a rabbit's digestive tract in as few as 5 hours. (Sakaguchi 1992) The cecum empties at a slower rate when dietary fiber drops below 14%.

If your rabbit is reluctant to eat the hay that's available to her at all times, try having two different kinds available alternately. This way you can give fresh offerings of one kind then the other, or even fresh offerings of the same hay. When I come around in the afternoon, and offer my rabbits the same kind of hay that they're sitting on, they grab it from my hand like it's a big deal.

MEDICAL TREATMENT

When the GI tract, upper or lower, has stopped moving, your veterinarian will look first at your rabbit's diet and the previously stated possibilities, as well as other causes—congenital deformations, adhesions, lesions, inflammations—anything that will makes passage difficult through the intestine. Sometimes other organs may affect or partially block the intestine.

Drugs, such as metaclopramide or cisapride, that stimulate intestinal motility, are sometimes used. Steroids (prednisone, winstrol) might be used if inflammation is involved. Antibiotics may be prescribed, if the veterinarian suspects a bacterial infection. Very often subcutaneous fluids are given and also pain medication, if needed.

HEALTH CLUES IN THE LITTERBOX

Watch the litterbox for what is coming through bunny's digestive tract. This will tell you a lot about what is going on inside him. You should see regular round dry marbles. You may also find some soft clusters of cecotropes. When excessive amounts of cecotropes are left unconsumed, it may mean that his diet is too protein rich (reducing the need for the protein-rich cecotropes). Try reducing pellets and giving extra low-protein, high-fiber grass hay. If dietary adjustment does not correct the problem, a veterinary exam is advisable, as there may be an illness involved. Cecotropes are often mistaken for diarrhea, but the shape and consistency should be noted. Diarrhea is an unformed or watery mass and is never a good sign in the litterbox.

Small hard scanty droppings means less is coming through. You need to find out why. Is less going in? Is the appetite poor? If the scanty droppings are strung together with thick hair, it may mean that hair is accumulating in the stomach.

Also, in the litterbox, you will notice a variation in urine color—from creamy white to dark orange, depending on what Bunny has been eating. People have been frightened unnecessarily by red urine caused by dietary changes, such as excess alfalfa or pine or fur twigs. This is usually what you are seeing as "red" urine.

In addition to watching what is coming through, watch how it is coming through. Is bunny straining? Does there appear to be any pain or discomfort? This is all useful information to report to your veterinarian in making a diagnosis. ∎

Hay and health: Lured into the litterbox with some timothy hay, Norman will leave all kinds of information about himself.

PHOTOGRAPH: BOB HARRIMAN

MICROBIAL INFECTIONS

ALTHOUGH SOME VIRUSES have been identified in rabbits, we are more often dealing with diseases that are caused by bacteria and protozoa (one-celled organisms, such as amoeba). Vaccines are not readily available for most of these. To complicate matters, some of the common microbes carried by other species are sometimes more pathogenic (harmful) to rabbits. Yet, many of us live in multi-animal households, and our animals lead long healthy lives.

Other than a few precautions, we don't take extreme measures. We practice reasonable house cleaning. A lot of loose dirt and dust should not be floating around where it can be inhaled by noses six inches from the floor, and exposure to other animals' excrement should be minimized. Cats and rabbits often share litterboxes, but if one or both animals run outdoors on the ground, the litterbox should be changed frequently. There is more chance of "bugs" being carried to the litterbox from outside.

AVOIDING EPIDEMICS

Among rabbits, many of their diseases are not as contagious as we once feared. Of course in our foster homes, we have to confront the possibility of contagious unapparent disease whenever we bring new rabbits home. We practice a two-week quarantine for incoming rabbits, but this is as much for their protection as for the rabbits already in residence. We like to allow incoming rabbits a little time to adjust to their new environment so that they won't be compromised by stress when they are exposed to household pathogens for the first time.

DEFENSES FROM WITHIN

An animal's immune system is usually able to defend against invading microorganisms by producing antibodies that destroy them. But when the animal is stressed, physically or psychologically, the immune

Multi-species household: *Living in reasonable cleanliness companion animals do not seem to infect each other.*

system is weakened, and then some of the more opportunistic pathogens can get a foothold.

Bacterial invasion may take one of several courses. The first (and worst) is that it may become septicemic and spread via the blood from a less critical location to a vital organ. (A toe abscess and pneumonia may be caused by the same bacteria.)

Another course is that the infection may become walled off where it can't be "seen" and destroyed by the immune system and where it can't be penetrated by antibiotics. A walled-off infection, or abscess, may eventually rupture and spill its contents into surrounding tissue and then become septicemic. Bacteria, from an abscess, may slip through small sinuses to form adjacent pockets of infection. Bacteria may set up a low-grade persistent infection of mucosal tissues. And, in some cases, the rabbit may eliminate the disease.

Certain protozoan infections also can cause problems in rabbits. Symptoms in some cases may be similar to bacterial infection, so adequate diagnostic testing is needed (see page 94).

ANTIBIOTIC THERAPY

The choice in drugs for most bacterial infections is simply made by culturing the bacteria and

"...a small blood sample can provide a very insightful window..."

finding their sensitivities. It's not so simple with a rabbit. Your veterinarian has to prescribe medication that will destroy the bacteria causing the infection, without destroying the intestinal bacteria necessary for your rabbit's digestion.

Bacteria are classified into two groups, gram-positive and gram-negative, by special stains. Both reside in the rabbit intestine, but drugs with predominantly gram-positive spectra can upset the bacterial balance. The most commonly used, potentially dangerous drug (to rabbits), taken orally, is Amoxicillin. Rabbits have died after sev-

eral days' or even one treatment with Amoxicillin. Even injectable penicillin should be used for only a short time (usually no more than 5 days), preferably along with gentamicin for a more balanced spectrum. Your veterinarian may hospitalize your rabbit to watch for toxic reaction.

Antibiotics are either bacteriostatic (stops the growth of multiplying bacteria) or bactericidal (stops metabolism within the bacterial cell and kills it). Both are used in rabbit treatment.

The goal in antibiotic therapy is to buy time until the immune system can take over the job of

Detecting Infection

BILL HARRIMAN

THERE ARE TWO BASIC APPROACHES to detecting infections of any sort, whether they be bacterial, viral, or protozoan. One is to go for the pathogen directly; the other is to demonstrate an immune response to the pathogen. Direct detection is useful when samples can be easily obtained, such as is the case with a bacteria-laden abscess. Culturing the bacteria can aid in identifying the strain, and it has the additional benefit of potentially providing antibiotic sensitivity information. Pathogens can sometimes be found in the blood, but in most cases their numbers are below the limit of detection.

In many instances infections are deep inside tissues, and direct detection is only feasible for post-mortem analysis. However, a small blood sample can provide a very insightful window to the status of the immune response. Because antibodies are soluble proteins, they float freely in the blood and can be easily detected even though the B cells which produce them, and the pathogen which induced the B cells to produce

them, may be tucked away in some hard-to-find tissue.

The most common technique for detecting serum antibodies to a particular pathogen is called enzyme-linked immunosorbant assay, or ELISA. Typically, a known antigen (whole pathogen or some component thereof) is bound to a plastic dish, followed by the addition of the test serum. If the serum contains antibodies to that particular antigen, they will bind to the antigen on the dish. The dish is washed and then a known species-specific antibody is added which binds to the serum antibodies from the first step (if any are present). The second antibody is linked to an enzyme which can convert an uncolored substrate to a colored compound. The intensity of the color reflects the relative amount of antigen-specific antibody in the serum.

This type of analysis is very sensitive and usually reliable, but requires an active immune response for detection. And again, it is an indirect demonstration of infection. Thus, false positives can occur (due to antibody cross-reactivity), but such cases are rare if the assay is performed properly. ∎

Bill Harriman holds a PhD in immunology from University of California, San Francisco.

destroying the infection. In rabbits, this can take several weeks, or even several months, especially when the infections are in the more difficult to reach areas, such as bony tissue, the nasal cavity, the brain, inner ear, lymph nodes or internal organs. These must be treated with a hardworking systemic antibiotic.

PROLONGED TREATMENT

As House Rabbit Society volunteers, we have rescued many rabbits who are terminally ill or chronically ill, but with proper care, they lead fairly normal lives. And we can extend these lives by months and years.

Dr. Carolynn Harvey's table (below) lists sev-

Useful Drugs for Rabbits

CAROLYNN HARVEY, DVM

ANTIBIOTIC

Group 1—Generally well tolerated, OK for prolonged use

Chloramphenicol: Oral suspension/subcutaneous injection. Possibility for severe reaction in sensitive *humans*; minimize your contact with drug.

Ciprofloxacin: Pills—can be hidden in a treat or crushed and suspended in liquid.

Enrofloxacin (*Baytril*): Pills/injection. Injectable liquid may be given orally. May cause joint problems in growing *dogs*; joint effects in young rabbits unknown.

Sulfa drugs (*Albon*): Oral suspension/pills/ in drinking water.

Tetracycline: Oral suspension/injection/in drinking water (bitter—may need to flavor water).

Trimethoprim/sulfa (*Diatrim, Bactrim*): Oral suspension only. Injectable form currently off market.

Group 2—Use with caution, or for limited periods

Ampicillin; Cephalosporins: Good penetration of infected tissue, effective against Pasteurella. Do not use orally—fatal diarrhea may result. Use injectable with caution. Stop if diarrhea or poor appetite is seen. Usually limit use to 5 days consecutive.

Amikacin; Gentamicin (*Gentocin*): Usually well tolerated. May cause kidney damage. Length of treatment limited by kidney concerns, usually 3–10 days. Adequate hydration is essential. Use under veterinary supervision.

Procaine Penicillin G: Injectable form usually well tolerated, but diarrhea can result. If diarrhea or poor appetite is seen, stop immediately. Usually limit use to 5 consecutive days.

Metronidazole (*Flagyl*): Effective against anaerobes.

Tilmicosin (*Micotil*): *Not* approved for use in rabbits. May cause sudden death in rabbits. *Very* effective against Pasteurella. Discuss pros and cons with your veterinarian. Injectable form only. *Not* safe for use in humans—avoid accidental exposure.

ANTIFUNGAL

Griseofulvin: Oral suspension. Teratogenic—should not be used in pregnant animals.

ANALGESICS

Aspirin (*not tylenol or other drugs such as ibuprofen*): Up to 50 mg per pound of rabbit twice a day by mouth. We find that $1/4$ to $1/2$ of a 325 mg tablet usually brings relief.

Buprenorphine: Injectable narcotic-type drug. Controlled substance, not for home use.

Butorphanol (*Torbutrol, torbugesic*): Injectable narcotic-type drug

Flunixin meglumine: Oral/injectable anti-inflammatory drug not approved for use in rabbits. Can cause GI bleeding in other species, usually well tolerated by rabbits, especially short term.

*Carolynn Harvey, **DVM** practices veterinary medicine in Oakland, California where she treats hundreds of rabbits a year.*

"Separate the lips with your thumb and stick the syringe in from the side."

eral drugs that she has found useful in her practice. Two major concerns with prolonged treatment are side effects (rarely encountered with drugs from Group 1) and bacterial resistance, a situation in which the bacteria we are trying to destroy become resistant to the antibiotic.

There is no fixed time for this to occur, and in our experience, resistance has not developed quickly in rabbits. Antibiotics still have a tough job because rabbits tend to wall off infections into areas that the antibiotic can't reach. Antibiotics vary in their ability to penetrate inflammatory tissue and pus. Most don't work very well, but they do help check any bacteria that may leak out of a walled-off abscess and thus prevent spread to the rest of the body. This may explain why the bacteria in a walled-off abscess may not become resistant to the antibiotic, even after very prolonged treatment. We have rabbits who have been on the antibiotic Baytril for years, and cultures of their bacterial infections still show sensitivity to Baytril.

GIVING MEDICINE

After your veterinarian decides which medicine to prescribe, it will be your job to give it. Oral suspensions are usually made up in tasty forms and don't present much of a problem. Getting yourself in the right positions is the main effort. One reason I encourage my rabbits to develop a taste for banana (in very small amounts because of calories) is that it's very easy to disguise medicine, should the need ever arise. Tablets can be crushed and mixed into some mashed banana or quartered and inserted into a slice like cloves into an orange.

If you need to force the issue, syringes are easier. Plastic oral syringes that come with your veterinary prescriptions for syrup-type medica-

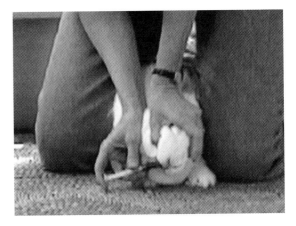

tion can also be used for tablets by cutting off the tips. You can squeeze some Nutrical or mashed banana into the syringe and surround the tablet chunks with something good tasting.

The easiest way to give an uncooperative rabbit medicine is on the floor. Approach a sleeping or relaxed rabbit from behind. Straddle the rabbit. Kneel down with your feet turned in (so he can't back out between your legs). Put a hand on top of the head, with your thumb on the side of the mouth. Separate the lips with your thumb and stick the syringe in from the side (between the teeth). Easy enough.

Injections can be given from the same straddled position, or from just about any position. Most rabbit injections are given at the tough and insensitive area at the scruff (over the shoulders). Rabbits are much easier to give injections to than cats, and usually they don't even know they've had a shot, especially if they're distracted with a treat at the same time. If your rabbit is given a prescription of injectable medication, you will be given adequate instructions by your veterinarian. ∎

VIDEOGRAPH: MARINELL HARRIMAN

"...rabbits may benefit from these special exams even more than other animals..."

To a Long Life: Geriatric Workups

ELIZABETH TESELLE

ALTHOUGH MOST VETERINARIANS routinely suggest geriatric exams for their older feline and canine patients, many may not be accustomed to doing the same for rabbits. However, rabbits may benefit from these special exams even more than other animals because they are such symptom hiders. Many serious diseases do not manifest signs until the organs or systems involved are too far gone for veterinary science to do much good, so getting the jump on them makes all the difference. In fact, something as simple as a white blood count can let you know if your rabbit is incubating an infection well before she experiences outward signs.

In our household, rabbits have "baseline" chemistries and CBCs run by the time they are two or three years old. Since most veterinarians and labs do not have access to reliable normal values for rabbits, the baseline serves as a measuring stick to which the veterinarian can compare future results. When our rabbits are four, we begin having bloodwork done once a year, and by the age of six, they are getting checked twice a year. We do a complete workup yearly, and at the six month point, perform a limited chemistry and CBC (which hit the "high points"). Since we began these geriatric workups, we have caught a number of potentially dangerous problems and were able to prevent or control them early.

Zoe's checkup: Dr. Cindy McBee of Nashville begins the procedure by drawing blood from Zoe's ear vein.

Urine samples can be difficult to obtain from rabbits, but having a baseline urinalysis done early on is also a good idea. To catch a urine sample, put the rabbit in a small empty cage with a wire floor. If possible, wrap the cage tray in a plastic bag before sliding it under the cage to ensure that the sample will remain as clean as possible.

Leave the rabbit in the cage until she urinates, being sure to check often to prevent the urine from becoming contaminated with feces. Use a syringe to remove the urine cleanly from the tray, and refrigerate the sample until you can take it to the vet (do this as soon as possible).

Of course, all this labwork is not much use if you don't know what you're looking for. Keeping an accurate chart that displays bloodwork results from year to year ensures that you and your vet can easily compare results and catch a slight change before it signals a major problem. These records can be kept in a booklet, a computer, or a file folder, but however you choose to organize your records, keep them as accurate and up-to-date as possible. If you must have labwork run at an emergency clinic, your records will be invaluable to the vet on call, who will appreciate immediate access to your rabbit's prior results.

Although geriatric exams for rabbits may be new to some veterinarians, most will be pleased that you want to provide the best in preventive medicine for your rabbit, and will be willing to work with you in obtaining normal values and analyzing the results of your rabbit's tests. ■

PHOTOGRAPH: ELIZABETH TE SELLE

CONDITIONS THAT REQUIRE TREATMENT

BECAUSE RABBITS HAVE NOT LIVED in human homes as long as dogs and cats, less is known about when their lives are in danger, how serious a problem is, and when to get emergency veterinary care. With dogs and cats you often have more time to "wait and see." For rabbits, waiting can be fatal. Here are a few conditions that require a judgment call.

ANIMAL ATTACKS

If your rabbit has been attacked by a dog, a raccoon, or any predatory animal, take him to the vet even if you see no bite wounds. These sometimes are unobservable without a veterinary exam. Also a bunny might experience shock that may not be apparent for several hours. Precautionary treatment for shock is advisable anytime a rabbit has been subjected to the trauma of an attack.

Topical eye drops: Perry's runny eyes are treated daily with ophthalmic solution. Ointments can also be used.

BLEEDING TOENAILS

When toenails grow too long, they can break off and bleed (that's why you keep them clipped short). This may not require rushing off to the vet, but it does require adequate cleaning with a disinfectant. Keep bunny confined on a clean surface until the bleeding has stopped. You may have to apply a styptic powder to stop the bleeding. If bone is exposed, antibiotics may be needed to prevent infection, so a veterinary exam is advised.

BLOODY URINE

This may indicate infection, urinary stones, or possibly cancer. To determine if it is truly blood in the urine, further veterinary testing will be needed. Be sure to review any recent dietary changes that may cause a reddening of the urine color.

CONJUNCTIVITIS

Runny eyes are not uncommon in rabbits. Many rabbits with runny eyes show no other signs of illness. There are a variety of causes including allergies and long-term low-pathogenic infection. External irritants may be involved, such as ammonia. Some rabbits may not have well developed tear ducts.

Culturing for bacterial infection is often difficult, so we normally treat topically, for a while, in case there is an infection. Your veterinarian may choose to flush the tear ducts with an antibiotic solution and prescribe an ophthalmic ointment for you to apply at home. If the apparent infection extends to other areas, your vet will undoubtedly start your bunny on systemic as well as topical antibiotics.

CUTS AND LACERATIONS

While house rabbits don't need extraordinary sanitation in their living environment (no more than other indoor animals), extra care is needed to keep household bacteria out of cuts or open wounds. Rabbits become infected quite easily and have a hard time dealing with infections. Always have a bottle of wound disinfectant (polyhydroxydine solution) on hand and use it immediately if bunny incurs a scratch. Keep any cut, scratch, laceration, or open wound clean and

"For an already compromised animal, a dip can be fatal."

check it daily for several days.

Deep cuts or large open, bleeding, or puncture wounds should be seen by the veterinarian. Stitches and antibiotics may be necessary.

DIARRHEA, CONSTIPATION, NO STOOLS

Diagnostic testing is needed to determine the cause. Accompanying behavior with any of these conditions will help determine how urgently veterinary care is needed. If bunny has diarrhea and is listless, rush him to the hospital. If he is constipated, bloated, and sitting in a scrunched up position, put your ear to his abdomen and listen. Too much sound or no gut sound at all are danger signals. Call your vet for an appointment.

EAR MITES

Noticeable signs are head and ear shaking. Inspection of the ear reveals dark scabby material inside it. Treat with mineral oil or a topical medication. Many of these are available in pet supply stores. Severely painful cases should be seen by a veterinarian so that a medication with a topical anesthetic can be prescribed.

The easiest way to get rid of ear mites is systemically with ivermectin, from your vet. Ivermectin can be given orally or by injection. One dose, followed by a second two weeks later will usually eliminate mites. Recheck often. They may still be in the environment.

FLEA INFESTATION

Control of fleas is normally a matter of upkeep. Flea infestation becomes a disease state when it is severe, and masses of black grains of "dirt" (actually dried blood)

are seen on the skin. Fleas can cause skin allergies, and prolonged severe infestation can result in loss of blood to the extent of causing anemia. This occurs especially among older less agile animals who are not able to groom themselves.

Severe flea infestations should be attacked aggressively—but this does not include a flea dip. For an already compromised animal, a dip can be fatal. And flea collars are lethal for rabbits who manage to chew them. Your best bet is to work with powders and a flea comb (see Grooming) and add an iron supplement to the diet.

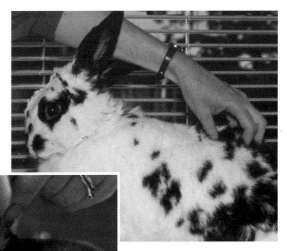

Checking evidence: *Peggy's ears (left) are examined for the crusty material that indicates ear mites. Phoebe's itchy spine (above) is checked for fleas. Flaky dandruff and hair loss can mean fur mites or flea allergy. You may not see fleas, but "flea dirt" tells you that they have dined on your bunny.*

"...plan a teeth-trimming program that works for you."

FLY STRIKE

Compromised animals are more vulnerable, but any rabbit with open wounds or a dirty bottom, may fall victim to egg-laying flies. Maggots not only cause damage by burrowing into flesh, but they also release toxins that can cause death.

If you find a fly stricken rabbit, take immediate action. If you are within 10 minutes of your veterinarian, go at once. If not, you can plunge the affected area under running tap water and wash them off yourself. You must still hurry to vet. There may be more larvae or eggs that you have not seen, and, your veterinarian will want to give fluids to detoxify your stricken bunny and treat for shock.

FUR MITES (CHEYLETIELLA)

Evidence is seen especially on the lower spine or across the shoulders where a thick layer of itchy flaky skin has developed. Often the clumps of hair will fall out along with the flakes of skin. Both flea allergies and fur mites cause these uncomfortable skin conditions. Both can be treated with flea powders. The active ingredient preferred by my veterinarians is carbaryl. Some of the natural (as opposed to the synthetic) pyrethrins may cause respiratory problems.

HEAD TILT

The cause is often a bacterial infection in the inner ear that affects the rabbit's balance. A vet exam and antibiotics are needed. Other causes might be parasitic disease in the brain or stroke.

HEAT STRESS

Bunny is panting and has a wet nose. During hot weather, your freezer should have milk or juice cartons full of ice ready to lay next to your hot bunny. Misting the ears with cool water can bring the temperature down. A wet towel across one end of the cage or playpen, with plenty of air blowing through, can make an evaporative cooler.

LUMPS, BUMPS

You needn't rush to the hospital in the middle of the night if you notice a lump on your normal-acting bunny. You should, however, make an appointment and have it checked soon. Abscesses and tumors can be serious, and treatment will depend on specifically what it is.

MALOCCLUSION

Whether due to hereditary factors or to injuries that pull the teeth out of alignment, some rabbits develop a malocclusion. This means that the teeth do not line up. They overgrow, and bunny can't eat.

Veterinarians have become experienced at treating this problem, so if you have a rabbit with maloccluded incisors or molars, it is best to discuss your options with your veterinarian and plan a teeth-trimming program that works for you. The condition does need to be treated or it can result in root and jaw infections, which are very difficult to reach with antibiotics.

Keep on smiling: *Teeth can be checked from the underside or from the "knee" position (page 63).*

VIDEOGRAPH: MARINELL HARRIMAN

"All respiratory symptoms should be evaluated by a veterinarian."

PARALYSIS

Partial or complete paralysis can be caused by: trauma to the head or back; strokes; tumors; toxins; viruses; bacterial and protozoan infections; nematodes; degenerative disease; or osteoporosis.

The most common cause of rabbit paralysis is a protozoan infection called encephalitozoonosis. Rabbits with loss of mobility should have a complete neurological exam and blood workup. Treatment and care depends on severity and specific cause. For long-term care see page 90.

RESPIRATORY CONGESTION

Noticeable symptoms are nasal discharge or sneezing. There may also be rattly or labored breathing. Labored breathing in a rabbit is not short panting but rather long hard breaths.

Some rabbits may be experiencing allergic reactions to bedding material, dust or cigarette smoke. The same symptoms may indicate long-term chronic upper-respiratory infections, or the onset of life-threatening illness. All respiratory symptoms should be evaluated by a veterinarian.

SEIZURES, COMA, STUPOR

Any time you find your rabbit unconscious, for any reason, it is a medical emergency, and you must rush your rabbit to the doctor. The cause may be electrocution, poisoning or a range of other possibilities. If you suspect poisoning, take any substance in question along with you.

SORE HOCKS, FOOT ABSCESSES

This is a perplexing problem not just limited to heavy rabbits with feet on wire. The fur on any rabbit's feet can wear down, exposing the skin and forming calluses. Rabbits can run about on hardwood or linoleum floors without injury to their callused feet. It's the sitting surface that matters. It must be dry. This includes all resting boards. If the litterbox is not changed daily, keep it topped with dry material so that the surface next to the feet is always dry.

Moisture-damaged skin is easily cracked, allowing dirt to penetrate. Dirt in an open foot-wound nearly always causes difficult-to-treat infections. Disinfect all open wounds with polyhydroxydine or chlorhexidine solution. If any swelling occurs within a day or two, take bunny to the vet. Antibiotics, bandages, and long-term treatment may be necessary.

STRAINING

Symptoms of urinary disorders may be first noticed in a series of little puddles around the litterbox instead of in it. You might notice excessive water drinking, or you may see bunny standing for some time in a urinating posture. Any of these symptoms warrant a veterinary exam.

Kidney/bladder stones and "sludge" urine are more common in rabbits than we had once realized. Restricting dietary calcium and vitamin-D may help. Urinary infection is often involved, and treatment usually requires antibiotics.

URINE SCALD

This may be an indication of kidney disease but more often it is a secondary problem in crippled, sick, or arthritic rabbits who are unable to posture (get into a position to project the urine away from the body). Urine-soaked fur keeps the skin constantly exposed to the irritating urine. The skin becomes inflamed, and usually the hair falls out. (See page 90 for treatment.)

WET CHEEKS

Wet fur on the cheeks under chronically runny eyes may irritate the skin and cause hair loss. Mild wetness can be blotted with tissue. Very wet and matted fur on the cheeks can be cleansed with ophthalmic saline solution, blotted, then flea combed for remaining debris. ∎

CARE OF THE YOUNG

Hand-raised orphans *from Hayward Animal Control prepare for adoption.*

A fur-lined "well." Make a well with your fist in the middle of the nestbox and fill it with fur from the mother. If she hasn't pulled out fur herself, clip some.

Babies. Group them into this "well of fur" (yes, you can handle them). They will burrow to the bottom and stay there until Mother Bunny stands over them to nurse them.

Mama Bunny. Show her where her babies are but don't expect her to get in there with them. Rabbits nurse once a day—usually very late at night or pre-dawn. Rabbit milk is very rich in protein and can sustain the babies for 24 hours. If you weigh the babies daily on a postal or kitchen scale and they are gaining weight, you can be sure that Mama Bunny is feeding them.

WHENEVER I RECEIVE a frantic phone call over an "accidental" litter of babies, I always give a lecture on spaying and neutering. Rabbits can get pregnant the day they give birth!

Now let's assume the accident has already taken place. A young adolescent mother in a bewildered state has just dropped a bunch of babies behind your kitchen door. You're unprepared, and the stores are closed. What to do?

NECESSARY INGREDIENTS

A nestbox (about 12x14 inches). Cardboard will do temporarily, but it will get soggy and have to be replaced. The bottom should have a couple of drain holes. The sides can be about 8 inches high, but the front should be no higher than 4 inches where Mama Bunny enters and exits.

Bedding. Line the box with a 3-inch layer of clean yellow straw or finely shredded paper.

THE ORPHANED LITTER

Hand raising is very difficult. Yet we have brought home many orphaned bunnies from animal shelters and raised them successfully by taking the following steps:

1. Set up a nestbox as described earlier

2. Obtain fur from any healthy rabbit (if that's not possible, use soft cotton rags or tissue).

3. Provide warmth. Several babies brood each other (share body heat), but one or two may need help. Keep the room temperature at 70° day and night and attach a heating pad to one side of an open nestbox. Remember, this is a small area that can overheat quickly. If you use a heating pad,

"...natural sucking motion closes the larynx and minimizes the danger of aspiration."

keep it to one side, set on low, and monitor it closely.

4. Wash faces and bottoms with warm water and cotton after every feeding. This is for cleanliness and also to help with elimination.

HAND FEEDING METHODS

You can bottle feed, syringe feed, or tube feed. Bottle feeding requires a perfect nipple. Carefully shave off some of the rubber at the end of the nipple. It's easier to punch the right size hole through thinner rubber. The hole should allow a very fine spray (neither huge nor tiny drops). Once you get a perfect nipple, bottle feeding is easy and should be done just twice a day.

Syringe feeding is messier because much of the formula dribbles down the chin and neck. The babies lap up the formula from the end of the syringe rather than draw with suction from a rubber nipple. Once you start them on syringes, you can't switch them to a bottle, because they lose their nursing reflex very quickly (within 2 days). Syringe feedings are more frequent (5-6 times a day) because less is consumed at a time.

The danger with hand feeding is that the liquid can get into the air passage and the baby may strangle or develop pneumonia. My own preference for nursing bottles is because the baby's natural sucking motion closes the larynx and minimizes the possibility of aspiration.

The windpipe is bypassed entirely by inserting a feeding tube directly into the stomach. This procedure is obviously not for a novice and should be done under veterinary supervision.

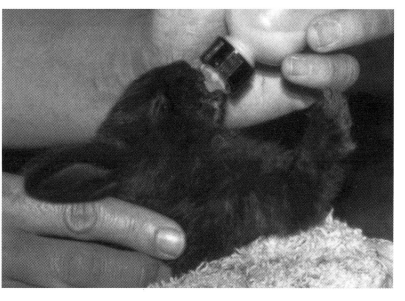

WHAT TO FEED

Canned kitten formula from the pet supply store is suitable for orphan rabbits. *Lactobacillis acidophilus* from a health-food store won't hurt and may be helpful for some babies. I include it.

Whether you feed twice or several times a day, this is the approximate daily total.

AGE	KMR	ACIDOPHILUS
Newborn	5 cc	1/2 cc
1 week	15-25 cc	1 cc
2 weeks	25-27 cc	1 cc
3 weeks	30 cc	2 cc
4 weeks	30 cc	2 cc

Bunnies can nibble on dry alfalfa and a few pellets as soon as they show interest—at 2-3 weeks. Formula consumption levels off at about 4 weeks, but don't rush weaning. ∎

CONVALESCENT CARE

Convalescing comfortably: *Lillian and Ashley (left to right) share a synthetic sheepskin rug after their surgeries.*

R ABBITS WHO ARE RECOVERING from an illness or injury, are chronically ill, or have simply grown old may require some special handling. Several diseases can leave a rabbit permanently disabled. Animals seem to have much less difficulty adjusting to loss of mobility than the humans who look after them do. Rabbits with crippling disease may stabilize and live comfortably for a prolonged period of time.

A convalescing rabbit often needs subcutaneous fluids. This not only keeps up hydration but it balances the electrolytes and helps flush out toxins. Lactated Ringer's Solution (LRS) is given for a number of conditions including: toxicity, kidney malfunction, fever, and digestive upsets. B-vitamins can be added to the bag of LRS for anorexic rabbits. This treatment can be done at home, after your veterinarian gives instructions.

LONG-TERM DISABILITIES

Millions of humans are on lifelong medication, for everything from allergies to heart disease, and no one questions their quality of life. We don't de-stroy humans who are missing a limb or have a physical impairment. Many kinds of infirmity do not involve pain, so let's be careful about judging from appearances alone. If you have learned your rabbit's body language, you can sense a will to live.

Does he enjoy his meals? Does he enjoy being petted? Does he turn his ears towards intriguing sounds? Are his eyes bright? Does he show interest when the cat walks by and in the things going on around him?

House Rabbit Society volunteers have lived with many invalid rabbits. Often these are especially wonderful animals. Don't be appalled by outward deformity. Inside may be a cheerful and well-adjusted bunny. If you have such an animal, there are ways to minimize your work. A disabled rabbit can no longer hop into the litterbox, so other arrangements have to be made.

INCONTINENCE/URINE BURN

The first thing that has to be dealt with in a crippled animal is incontinence. This is probably a misnomer, since the problem is not always loss of bladder control but rather a posturing problem that results in urine-soaked hindquarters and consequent urine burn.

A routine is needed for keeping urine off bunny's skin. First dip the area in plain lukewarm water (or hold under a tap of running water) to wash the urine off. Pat dry. You can then use an ointment treatment or a powder treatment, never both at the same time. With ointment, apply an anti-inflammatory antibiotic ointment, if the skin is badly inflamed, or petroleum jelly to prevent moisture from getting into the area. With powder treatment you try to keep the scalded

PHOTOGRAPH: TANIA HARRIMAN

"We consider this kind of stabilization a huge success."

area dry by applications of talcum powder or baking soda.

Depending on the degree of immobility, two options are available. Diapers (newborn size) are marvelous for an incontinent rabbit. Just as with human children, they draw the moisture away from the tender flesh. We had several different rabbits in diapers for over a year, and they never suffered urine burn. A partially mobile rabbit in diapers can scoot around on the floor freely and be part of the family without soiling rugs.

CUSHIONED COMFORT

A completely immobile rabbit can be kept on synthetic-sheepskin rugs that allow the moisture to drain away from the flesh. Use only rugs without a rubber backing (no bath mats). You don't want to trap the moisture inside the rug, next to your rabbit's skin. If bunny's rug is on the floor, put newspapers underneath it.

Washable rugs allow moisture to drain away from the bunny, but they do not blot wet fur the way diapers do. However, part-time use of a rug is the best solution for people who are away at work all day. Diapers should be changed at 4-6 hour intervals. Obviously, this can't be done in the middle part of the day, if no one is home. During this time, leave the diaper off and switch to the rug method. Bunny's bottom will probably need to be rinsed before you put a diaper on him in the evening.

FEEDING TECHNIQUES

Some disabled rabbits are able to feed themselves. Most drink more easily from a water bottle than a bowl. If bunny's digestion is impaired, or if chewing is a problem, hand feeding may be necessary, at least part of the time. It's not difficult once you get a strategy worked out. The following formula was devised to be consumed by a 6-pound rabbit within a 24-hour period:

1. Soak ½ cup dry pellets *in 1 cup water.
2. Run through a blender at medium speed for 5-10 minutes. (This is the right consistency for a feeding syringe.) After mixture is blended, you can add any extras that your veterinarian advises.

The amount of pellet "slurry" or "paste" that can be fed at one time is about 50 cc (for a 6-pound rabbit). Your vet can provide you with large feeding syringes. Once bunny is accustomed to the pellet paste, you can get him to lap it up from a small dish (⅓ cup is about 50 cc). A combination of feeding techniques can be used, by setting out less-perishable produce and hay for the times you cannot be there to hand feed. Then you can give supplemental feedings of the pre-mixed "pellet slurry" in the evening when you are home.

On a long-term basis, it is usually difficult to keep a compromised bunny's weight and hydration up, without the additional pellet slurry.

A JOB WELL DONE

Your last responsibility to your invalid is to provide entertainment. Remember how he has entertained you all of his life. Talk to him. Pet him. Move him around to different locations so that he doesn't get bored. Spend quality time. These are precious moments, and someday you will be grateful that you had this time.

A surprise discovery is that many chronically-ill rabbits can live comfortably and show a will to live for an extended period of time. When pain is not involved, we consider this kind of stabilization a huge success. It is unfortunate that many veterinarians regard these incurables as failures and automatically assume that euthanasia is the best choice for all crippled rabbits. We have reason to believe otherwise.   ∎

These pellets bulk at 4 cups per lb. For higher density pellets, use less than 1/2 cup. Use more water for slurry; less water for paste.

POWER OF THE PSYCHE

SOMETHING VERY SELDOM mentioned in veterinary manuals but acknowledged by experienced rabbit veterinarians is the importance of dealing with the rabbit psyche. Generally, this is thought to be accommodated in the veterinarian's "bedside manner"—soothing and sweet talking the rabbit into calmness. This may work quite well while the veterinarian is in the room, but what about the rest of the time a rabbit is being treated or hospitalized?

In caring for quite a few "sanctuary" rabbits with long and short-term illnesses, we have seen some miracles of motivation. We are convinced that friendship therapy contributes to the recovery or at least the stabilization of sick rabbits.

MIND OVER MATTER

We had a peculiar case with our 8-year-old Jefty. His depression over losing his mate to cancer triggered abnormal fur chewing. A good part of his body was suddenly bald, and a veterinary exam revealed that most of that hair was in his stomach. It seemed very unlikely that the huge mass would ever break up and pass. We started him on the "hairball" remedies and tried to stabilize him enough to survive surgery. Meanwhile, I added one more remedy to the treatment.

Friendship therapy:
Assisting the antibiotics, Octavia is credited for saving Phoebe's life, after pulling her through a 2-day crisis with pneumonia.

I introduced him to 10-year-old Sieglinda, who had recently lost her partner.

We postponed the surgery a few more days since the pair was bonding so well, and we wanted to give Jefty all the morale boosters he could get before the risky surgery. By the end of those few days, his improvement was so remarkable that we decided to wait and see. The fur mass was still in his stomach, but it was smaller.

I won't try to claim that getting happy cured a furball. But I will claim that it gave Jefty a reason to eat the hay and greens in front of him. He had someone to dine with and to share his pineapple cocktails with. In the next few weeks, this bald anoretic "skeleton" of a rabbit regained his handsome figure. Rechecks during the past year have shown that the furball is still decreasing in size. The only *physical* treatment given since the first two weeks has been the continuation of his high roughage diet.

A strong argument for looking at the psychological as well as the physical animal is that, yes, physical things must take place in the cure, but a mental incentive can sometimes be the button that sets those physical things in motion.

FOR PRACTICAL PURPOSES

Of course we don't introduce contagiously-sick rabbits into a new group, but separating bonded rabbits, after they become ill, does more harm than good. We have never separated bonded mates from their afflicted companions, and we

PHOTOGRAPH: MARINELL HARRIMAN

"...we have seen some miracles of motivation."

have never lost one to the same illness. If your rabbit is struggling for life and a cherished companion is nearby, the last thing you want to do is separate them. I keep bonded pairs together even if the sick rabbit must be hospitalized.

This is *routine* in Dr. Carolynn Harvey's practice, and we urge veterinarians everywhere to follow this wonderful example. The entire hospital staff knows that whenever a House Rabbit Society member checks in a critically ill rabbit who is one of a bonded pair, a second rabbit will be checked in for moral support. That's just part of the treatment.

Credit for our rabbits' survival must be given to excellent veterinary care, but the psyche factor is an additional tool in the doctor's bag of tricks and it may at times mean the difference between life and death. ■

PHOTOGRAPH: AMY ESPIE

NOTES

REFERENCES

Ayars, Garrison H. et al. 1989. The toxicity of constituents of cedar and pine woods to pulmonary epithelium. *Journal of Allergy Clinical Immunology* 83:610-618

Brooks. D. L., et al. 1993. Cage Enrichment for Female New Zealand White Rabbits. *Lab Animal* 30

Buddington, R. and J. Diamond. 1990. Ontogenetic development of monosaccharide and amino acid transporters in rabbit intestine. *American Journal of Physiology* 259:G544-55

Brown, Susan A. 1995. Internet discussion on "Motility of the Gastrointestinal Tract." Midwest Bird and Exotic Animal Hospital, Westchester, IL., April 19.

Cheeke, P.R. 1987. *Rabbit Feeding and Nutrition.* Orlando: Academic Press

Cunliffe-Beamer, T. L, Freeman, L. C., Myers, D. D. 1981. Barbiturate sleeptime in mice exposed to autoclaved or unautoclaved wood beddings. *Laboratory Animal Science* 31: 672–75

Fraga, M. 1990. Effect of type of fibre on the rate of passage and on the contribution of soft feces to nutrient intake of finishing rabbits. Journal of Animal Science 69:1566-74

Gidenne, T. 1992. Effect of fibre level, particle size and adaptation period on digestibility and rate of passage as measured at the ileum and in the faeces in the adult rabbit. British Journal of Nutrition. 67: 133-46

Lebas, F. (1980). Les recherches sur l'alimentation du lapin: Evolution au cours de 20 dernieres annees et perspectives d'avenir. Adapted by P. Cheeke1987. *Rabbit Feeding and Nutrition.* Academic Press

Perch, D.H. and S.W. Barthold. 1993. Pp. 179-80 in *Pathology of Laboratory Rodents and Rabbits* Ames, IA: Iowa State University Press

Sakaguchi, E. 1990. Digesta retention and fibre digestion in brushtail possums, ringtail possums and rabbits. Comparative Biochemistry and Physiology 96A:351-54

Vesell, E. S. 1967. Induction of drug metabolizing enzymes in liver microsomes of mice and rats on softwood bedding. Science 157: 1057-58

Wagner, J.L. 1974. Spontaneous deaths in rabbits resulting from gastric trichobezoars. Laboratory Animal Science 24:826-30

FURTHER READING

The Biology and Medicine of Rabbits and Rodents by John E. Harkness and Joseph E. Wagner,

A Practitioner's Guide to Rabbits and Ferrets by Jeffery R. Jenkins, DVM and Susan Brown, DVM

Rabbit Health News P.O. Box 3242, Redmond, WA 98073.

Journal of Small Exotic Animal Medicine, P.O. Box 618686, Orlando, FL 32861-8686.

FURTHER INFORMATION

(Nonprofit organizations appreciate a S.A.S. envelope)

YOUR LOCAL HUMANE SOCIETY OR SPCA provides excellent information and many sponsor rabbit rescue clubs.

HOUSE RABBIT SOCIETY (HRS) is a national nonprofit rescue organization with literature on rabbit health and behavior. P.O. Box 1201, Alameda, CA 94501. 510/521-4631.

HOME FOR UNWANTED AND ABANDONED GUINEA PIGS in Lawrenceville, Georgia. For care and behavior information, call 404/963-4755.

NATIONAL ANIMAL POISON CONTROL CENTER, a nonprofit organization, offers phone consultation with veterinarians trained in clinical toxicology, who know species differences in susceptibility to poisons. Fees are charged 1-900-680-0000 or 1-800-548-2423.

DIAGNOSTIC SERVICES

UNIVERSITY OF MISSOURI. ELISA tests for certain protozoal infections: Veterinarians can call 800/669-0825.

UNIVERSITY OF WASHINGTON. ELISA testing for Pasteurella: call Dr. Barbara Deeb 206/685-3202 or Julie Stewart 206/543-3074 for information.

ON-LINE INFORMATION

HRS WORLD WIDE WEB (WWW)
http://www.psg.lcs.mit.edu/~carl/paige/HRS-home.html

HOUSEBUN MAILING LIST
Send a message to: HouseBun-Request@webcom.com

INDEX